PEARSON   ALWAYS LEARNING

Elaine Austin-Tise

The Power of Words

Custom Edition for Arkansas Tech University

D1194590

Pearson Learning Solutions, 501 Boylston Street, Suite 900, Boston, MA 02116
A Pearson Education Company
www.pearsoned.com

Printed in the United States of America

000200010270752519

RR/JG

ISBN 10: 1-256-09156-1
ISBN 13: 978-1-256-09156-1

Table of Contents

Supplemental Lists

*Introduction

The Power of Words

Courtesy of the Everett Collection. Copyright © 20th Century Fox Film Corp.

Gene Wilder as Dr. Frankenstein in
Mel Brooks' *Young Frankenstein*

"A More Sophisticated Way of Expressing Myself"

In Mel Brooks' comedy *Young Frankenstein*, he reinforces a sometimes overlooked fact that words have power. This humorous parody of Mary Shelly's original *Frankenstein* demonstrates how words can affect the way we perceive ourselves and can change even the course of our lives. In Brook's version of this film and literary classic, Gene Wilder plays a young Dr. Frankenstein who insists that everyone pronounce his name "Fronkensteen." The young doctor is trying desperately to escape the negative connotations that his name evokes. When he finally embraces his heritage and decides to follow in his grandfather's footstep, he forcefully proclaims, "My name is *Frankenstein.*" The word "Frankenstein" no longer embarrasses him but makes him feel empowered. Therefore, he, like his grandfather before him, decides that he will create life. He asks his assistant Igor to steal the brain of a brilliant scientist in hopes that this will make his own experiment of playing God a success, unlike his grandfather who failed so miserably. However, Igor has a mishap with the "brilliant brain" and instead steals the brain of someone whom he tells Dr. Frankenstein is named *"Abby Normal."* Naturally, Dr. Frankenstein is *somewhat* upset at finding out that he has implanted an *"abnormal"* brain into an eight-foot giant. Igor's lack of vocabulary has created a *slight* problem. In other words, what do you do with an eight-foot giant with an abnormal brain? Dr. Frankenstein has, like his

1

grandfather, created a Monster who cannot communicate his thoughts and frustrations, which leads the Monster to act violently.

Dr. Frankenstein decides that the only responsible solution is to give the Monster half of his own "*normal*" brain. The tension builds as the terrified townspeople burst through the doors of the laboratory to destroy the Monster just as he is receiving part of his creator's brain. The Monster has always lived defensively and has always been misunderstood, acting violently because he cannot verbally express his hidden terrors; however, this time when confronted by the wrath of the townspeople, he does not roar fearfully and unintelligibly; instead, he eloquently states his feelings and thoughts, and the citizens' response is to accept him into their community, which drastically alters the Monster's life for the better. The only thing in his life that has changed is that young Dr. Frankenstein has given him "a somewhat more sophisticated way of expressing [himself]" (*Young Frankenstein*).

Courtesy of The Kobal Collection. Copyright © 20th Century Fox Film Corp.

How does this apply to you? Although you will probably never have anyone run away from you in abject terror, if you are unable to express your thoughts adequately, you will face unnecessary rejections; employers will turn you down for jobs; your scores in college will suffer, which may even result in your not getting a degree and, like the frustrated Monster, you may react with anger to a complex problem because you do not have the vocabulary to effectively express your thoughts. By increasing not just your vocabulary but also your awareness of language and how it functions, you can empower yourself, which will open doors of opportunity that would have otherwise remained closed. Just as it did for the Monster, increasing your vocabulary and knowledge of language can affect the course of your life in a positive way.

Getting Started

One of the first obstacles that students usually have to overcome is to understand the difference between the language they use within their own social or family structure and the language they need to use in college or in the workplace. The relationship between academic language and your own personal dialect is similar to table manners. The table manners you use, let's say, at McDonalds and the table manners you use at a formal dinner are different. Likewise for many students, so too is the language they will use throughout life when speaking to their friends or family as opposed to the language they will use when addressing their bosses or college professors. Please always remember, even when using your own dialect, you should not use incorrect grammar. No matter to whom you are speaking, you do not want to sound uneducated.

Why, you may ask, can't everyone just speak the same way I do? The world is developing into a more compressed global community where instant communication, worldwide news coverage, and the frequency of people traveling lead many to believe that dialects or accents belong to the past; however, this is not the case because each area of the country still has its own way of speaking. In other words, dialects are still alive and well. According to dialectologists, "in some major dialectical sections of the country, such as the North, Midland, and the South, dialects are actually diverging — not becoming more similar" (Rickerson).

This point is important because without the common language that standardized English provides, our country would over time become fragmented as each section developed its own special language, and ultimately, communication between even states would become difficult, if not impossible. As an example, let's look at a dialect used in Pittsburg, Pennsylvania, coined "*Pittsburghese.*" People living outside this geographical area would not realize that if someone called them "*nebby*" they were actually being told they were *nosey*. People might be alarmed or insulted if someone asked them if they wanted to "*jag off*," which simply means would you like to "*goof off*." If you are driving on the shoulder of the road, you would call it a "*berm.*" The relationship between the words *nebby/nosey, jag off / goof off,* and *berm / shoulder of the road* means the same thing; however, depending on which area of the United States you live, the vocabulary you use to describe them will vary. This is only one example of the millions of words that people say differently, depending on their dialect.

Because standardized English denotes words by their formal spelling and meaning, our newspapers, newscasts, and textbooks are understood by people from all sections of the country. People take this luxury for granted in the United States. Many countries do not even have a common newspaper that citizens located in different areas of their country can read and understand. Because of standardized English, the U.S.

enjoys the best of both worlds. Each community or area of the country can still express its own cultural uniqueness through an individualized dialect while still reaping the benefits of standardized English, which can be understood by all.

This workbook uses a holistic approach. Memorizing a word's definition is not enough. Before you can adequately use words in real-life conversations, you must know how words function in sentences, whether they are nouns, verbs, adjectives, or adverbs — and be able to use them in context. We will also look at ways to increase your reading speed by learning how to recognize context clues. Another area of focus will be how to break down words into parts in order to examine their meaning and etymology (history or origin).

This course is designed to help you gain a command of the English language that will not only help you attain your educational goals but will also help you function throughout your life. You only need to have one disputed warranty claim to realize that being able to effectively communicate your side of the issue can help you save perhaps thousands of dollars. Even in your personal life, if you are able to articulate your thoughts and emotions, interpersonal miscommunications are easier to resolve amicably (peacefully).   Therefore, this is not simply a course to help you while you are in college but to also help in every aspect of your life.

Techniques to Help You Learn Vocabulary

In each workbook exercise, you will be asked to look up a list of vocabulary words. You will write *the word, its phonetic spelling, its part of speech, its etymology, and its definition. You will also write a sentence using the word.*

Pronunciation:

Most students are nervous about using a new word during a conversation for fear they will say it incorrectly; however, learning how to use a pronunciation key should help alleviate (relieve) this fear since pronunciation keys help you sound out the word.

Let's look at the word *indomitable.*

/ / /
indomitable [ĭn-dŏm′ ĭ-tə-bəl)]; adj., (Latin) that which cannot be subdued or overcome; unconquerable; unyielding

Example sentence: The warrior has an indomitable spirit.

First you have the actual spelling of the word *indomitable* and directly following it is the pronunciation key or phonic spelling. The word is divided into syllables or word parts (*in-dom-i-ta-able*). The word part *"in"* has a short vowel for *'i'* and is noted with the symbol *"ĭ."* The *"o"* in the word part *"dom"* has a short vowel *"o,"* which the phonetic spelling denotes with an *"ŏ."*

Your first question may be, "How do I know how to make those particular sound?" *Example One* is a sample pronunciation key from the *American Heritage Dictionary.* In the second column of the pronunciation key, the lexiconist has listed the word *"pit"* for the corresponding sound for the symbol *"ĭ,* and *"pot"* as the corresponding sound to the symbol for *"ŏ."*

In next letter *"i"* is once again noted with the symbol *"ĭ,"* which indicates that it is has the short vowel sound. The next word part you need to note is *"tə."* The pronunciation key notes the corresponding sound for *"ə "* in the words *"about, item, editable, etc."* Now sound out the word *indomitable* using the sounds from the pronunciation key.

ĭn	=	p*i*t
dŏm	=	p*o*t
ĭ	=	p*i*t
tə	=	*a*bout
bə	=	*a*bout

Pronunciation Exercise

Use the pronunciation key in *Example One* and sound out the following words:

1. dĭ - spōz′
2. măg′ nəm
3. sĭn - thĕt′ ik
4. sprā
5. vī - ə - lĭt
6. slōp

Use the pronunciation key in *Example One*, write down the phonetic spelling from the pronunciation key, and sound out the following words:

1. articulate
2. benign
3. acclaim
4. denounce
5. frigid
6. iconic
7. indefensible
8. solstice
9. consumption
10. quench

Example One
American Heritage Dictionary

A list of the pronunciation symbols used in this Dictionary is given below in the column headed **AHD.** The column headed **EXAMPLES** contains words chosen to illustrate how the **AHD** symbols are pronounced. The letters that correspond in sound to the **AHD** symbols are shown in boldface. Although similar, the **AHD** and **IPA** (International Phonetic Alphabet) symbols are not precisely the same because they were conceived for different purposes.

The American Heritage® Dictionary of the English Language, Fourth Edition. 2000.

Pronunciation Key

EXAMPLES	AHD	EXAMPLES	AHD
pat	ă	boot	o͞o
pay	ā	out	ou
care	âr	pop	p
father	ä	roar	r
bib	b	sauce	s
church	ch	ship, dish	sh
deed, milled	d	tight, stopped	t
pet	ĕ	thin	th
bee	ē	this	th
fife, phase, rough	f	cut	ŭ
gag	g	urge, term, firm, word, heard	ûr
hat	h	valve	v
which	hw	with	w
pit	ĭ	yes	y
pie, by	ī	zebra, xylem	z
pier	îr	vision, pleasure, garage	zh
judge	j	about, item, edible, gallop, circus	ə

kick, cat, pi**que**	k	butter	ər
lid, need**le** <u>l</u>	l(nēd′l)		
mum	m		
no, sudden<u>l</u>	n(sŭd′n)		
thi**ng**	ng		
pot	ŏ	**FOREIGN**	**AHD**
toe	ō	*French* **feu**, *German* sch**ö**n *French* **oeuf**, *German* zw**ö**lf	œ
caught, paw, for, horrid, hoarse <u>2</u>	ô	*French* **tu**, *German* **ü**ber	ü
noise	oi	*German* i**ch**, *German* a**ch**, *Scottish* lo**ch**	KH
too**k**	o͝o	*French* bon (bôᴺ) <u>3</u>	N

(Answers to practice phonetic spelling exercise: dispose, magnum, synthetic, spray, violet, slope)

Definition of the Word

Although for the worksheet exercises, you are required to write down only the first definition of the assigned words, it is, nevertheless, important to note that the word may have multiple meanings.

For example, let's look at the word humor and its meanings:
humor (hyōō′mə r) n. 1. The quality of being amusing or comical: He saw humor in the situation. 2. The ability to perceive, enjoy, or express what is comical or funny: a sense of humor. 3. In medieval physiology, one of the four fluids of the body, blood, phlegm, choler, and black bile, the dominance of which was thought to determine a person's character and general health. [Middle English, *fluid*, from Old French umor, from Latin ūmor, hūmor.]

The first definition deals with the "quality" of actually "being" amusing or comical, and the second defines it as "[T]he ability to perceive, enjoy, or express" humor (*American*). Both of these definitions are similar in that they refer to comical humor; however, the third definition is quite different. It refers to a medieval physiology where a person's personality and moods were determined by the balance of fluids (blood, phlegm, choler, and black bile) or humors in a person's body.

Although this information seems anachronistic (out-of-date) compared to our modern ideas of physiology; nevertheless, at some point in your college career, you may study Shakespeare or some other Renaissance or medieval writer where this information will be important to your not only understanding a piece of literature but also your appreciation of it. Without this knowledge, you would assume that when Shakespeare refers to "humors," he is referring to something comical, which is incorrect. A perfect example is Shakespeare's Prince Hamlet who is controlled by the humor "black bile." According to physicians during the medieval and Renaissance's era, if black bile was the dominate fluid, the person would have a melancholy or depressed outlook on life, which is why scholars always refer to Prince Hamlet as the "melancholy Dane."

Every college student should keep a college-level dictionary handy during their studies. It not only gives the exact definition of a particular word but will also give you information on other ways you can use the word.

Using Vocabulary in Sentences:
Once you know the definition of the word, you are required to write a sentence using the word correctly. If you cannot use a word correctly in the context of a

9

sentence, you have not learned the word. You are merely parroting a definition and possibly the spelling, which will be of no use to you in real-life applications.

Types of Dictionaries:

There are two types of dictionaries, *unabridged* and *abridged*. An *unabridged* dictionary is complete and has not been condensed. An abridged dictionary, which is the type of dictionary that is usually included with your reading book, is a condensed version, meaning that words have been removed. Abridged dictionaries are the most common form of dictionaries because of their ease of handling and transporting.

The *Oxford Dictionary of English* is one of the most important dictionaries. It contains over 180,000 definitions of words, and during one year alone, it added more than 3,000 new words. The English language is a living language, meaning that it grows by continually adding new words. Words that have been recently added to dictionaries because they are so widely used are *spam, chat room, e-commerce,* and *cyberspace.*

When a language stops growing, it is called a dead language; Latin is an example of a dead language. Although many of our own English language is derived from Latin word parts and we also have the Romance languages which are direct descendents of Latin and include French, Spanish, Portuguese, Italian, and Romanian, Latin, however, as a *uniform language*, which bound together the Roman Empire, began to diminish after the fall this vast empire during the fifth century.

Definition Exercise

Look up the definition for each of the following words:

1. boycott

2. laconic

3. chauvinism

4. maverick

5. cynic

6. tantalize

7. Darwinism

8. Vandal

9. Machiavellian

10. Utopian

11

How to Recognize the Part of Speech

Parts of Speech:

It is important to recognize a word's part of speech or, in other words, what the word's function in the sentence is because depending on whether it is an adjective, adverb, noun, or verb, the spelling and pronunciation could change.

> *indomitable* [in-dŏm′ i-tə-bəl)]; ***adj.***, (Latin) that which cannot be subdued or overcome; unconquerable; unyielding
>
> /
>
> *Example sentence*: The warrior had an ***indomitable*** spirit.

> ***Indomitable*** describes *spirit,* which is a noun; therefore, indomitable is an adjective.

> *The part-of-speech labels are as follows:*

adj.	*adjective*	*indef. art.*	*indefinite article*
adv.	*adverb*	*interj.*	*interjection*
v.	*verb*	*conj.*	*conjunction*
n.	*noun*	*prep.*	*Preposition*
def. art.	*definite article*	*aux.*	*auxiliary*

A word's part of speech is important because depending on whether it is a *noun, verb, adjective, or adverb*, its function, spelling, and pronunciation may vary.

The word *tenacity* is a noun. If you want to use it as an adjective, it would be spelled *tenacious*. In addition, its pronunciation also varies slightly. Following is a brief explanation that may help you recognize a word's part of speech.

Simplified and Partial Guide to Part of Speech Recognition

(Partial List of Parts of Speech: Nouns, Verbs, Adjectives, and Adverbs):

Nouns:
- are *a person, place, thing, or idea*
- are capable of being made plural (two cars); possessive singular (Jim's car); possessive plural (Jim and Mary's cars)
- are derived from other words by the addition of the noun suffixes:

al	ance, ence	er, or	ion	ation
ity, ty	ment	ness	ure	

- can fit into the noun phrase

the _____   his _____   this _____

  Example: The *student* placed <u>two</u> *satchels* in <u>his</u> *locker*.
  <u>This</u> *watermelon* is ripe.

"Words which typically precede nouns are *a, an, the, my, your, his, her, its, our, their, this that, some, both, several, etc.* Theses words are called determiners. *Determiners* appear at the beginning of a noun phrase before any other modifiers. The following words belong to the class of *determiners:*

1. *the*
2. *a, an*
3. *my, our, your, his, her its, their*
4. *this, that, these, those*
5. *each, every, either, neither, another, other, any, certain, some, both, several, all, few, enough, many, more, most, much, little, less, no, other, such*
6. *whose, what, which*
7. *one, two, three, etc., and first, second, third, etc.*

Nouns can be divided into common nouns (those that point out a class of objects) and proper nouns (those that point out specific person, places, things, groups, etc.)

Adjectives
- describes or modifies a noun
- can also be comparative or superlative degree inflections and can be changed into a noun by adding the suffix –ness. (**Superlative degree**= comparison of the highest degree — brightest, greatest: **Comparative degree** = comparison of the intermediate degree — better, more beautiful)
- Following are suffixes which will also help you recognize an adjective.

ous	able	some	en	ive
y	ic	ish	ular	ful

Adverbs:
- *modifies verbs, adjectives, or other adverbs.*
- *Following are suffixes which will also help you recognize adverbs.* (Note: adding an ly to an adjective forms an adverb of manner)

ly	ward	wards	ways	wise

- Text frame for adverbs:
  "He exercised _____." "He lived _____." "He walked _____."

Verbs:
- *can be classified into three categories: transitive, intransitive, and linking.*

Examples:

1. *An intransitive verb* *does not need an object or complement to complete the sentence.*
   Subject- Intransitive Verb (S IntrV):
   S   IntrV
   Joseph wept.

2. *A transitive verb* *requires an object to complete the statement. A direct object can be identified in a sentence by asking the question What? Or Whom? following the subject and the verb.*

   Subject-Transitive Verb-Direct Object (S TvV DO)
   S   TrV   DO
   Samuel threw the ball.

   Note: *Always find the verb of the sentence first, which in this sentence is "threw." To find the subject of the sentence, ask yourself, "Who threw the ball." The answer would be Samuel. Once you have established the subject and verb use the following test to check to see whether the verb is a transitive verb. — Samuel Threw What?*
   Since you can logically answer the question with "ball," you know that "ball" is the direct object of the sentence and that the verb "threw" is a transitive verb.

3. **Linking verbs** *link the subject to its complement, which will be a noun (substantive or adjective) and will rename or describe the subject.*
   S LV SC
   Jane is tired.
   Jane grew tired.

Linking verbs are usually "to be" verbs (am, are, was, were, being, been, be), sense verbs (smell, taste, hear, etc.), or words such as become, remain, feel, seem, etc. (Schrock 15-26).

Knowing how to use a word such as *tenacity* correctly in a sentence is imperative (important) because if you use the noun form in the adjective function, the sentence will be incorrect. An analogy for the way open class words change functions within a sentence would be the way that you are a son or daughter, a student, and possibly an employee. You are the same person; however, the way you behave or "function" in each situation is different.

The word functions that we have just studied (noun, verb, adjective, and adverb) are called *open classes* of words because they can change their function within a sentence. *Closed classes* (preposition, articles, conjunctions, pronouns) never change their function within a sentence.

Look at the following nonsense sentence, and underline the noun, adjective, verb, and adverb in the sentence. You may want to refer to the partial list of part of speech recognition on pages 13 – 14.

The boglishous nibbledebuck rished bodashously toward the giglic bolderdash.

Exercise for Parts of Speech

Name of the part of speech (Noun, Adjective, Adverb, or Verb) for the underlined word in the following sentences:

1._____ His *laconic* way of speaking was wonderful.
2. _____I wish we lived in a *utopian* society, but unfortunately, we don't.
3._____ Don't *tantalize* me.
4._____ James is a *maverick* when he drives.
5. _____The *boycott* lasted for three weeks.

Exercise: *Look up the following words and write the different functions that you find, such as noun, verb, adverb, or adjective. Write a sentence using each word in its different function. (Function = how the word is functioning in the sentence: noun, adjective, adverb, or verb.)*

1. embarrassment

2. perceive

3. create

4. tension 紧张

5. intelligent

16

Origin of a Word (Etymology)

In most dictionaries, lexiconists also note the origin of a word or *etymology*, which usually follows the part of speech label. One may wonder why the pronunciations of English words vary so much from the way they are spelled. This is partly due to the etymology or history of words.

For example, let's look at the word *cereal*. Why is *cereal* not spelled the way it sounds, "sîr′ē-əl?" It is because of its etymology. The word *cereal* is taken from the name of the Roman goddess *Ceres,* the goddess of grain. To retain the history of the word's origins, the original "*cere*" remains as part of the spelling of *cereal*. Also by adding the suffix "*ist,*" we form another word "cerealist," which means a person who specializes in the study of grain. (*Dictionary.com*)

Without realizing it, people also recycle words. Our present internet generation may feel unique when we use the word "Email." However, this word was first coined by Ralph Waldo Emerson (1803-1882). Of course, Emerson was not speaking of it as a way of sending his writings to his editor since he could not even have telephoned his editor. Instead Email meant enamel, as in the glossy paint. In fact, the word *émailler* still means "to enamel" in French.

By knowing a word's history, you can understand why a word is spelled a certain way, and you can recognize or at least form an idea of what a derivative word (a word formed from another by derivation) means simply by knowing its history. A word's etymology at times also reveals how much language changes over time. When reading any dated material, a reader must take into consideration the time period the piece was written and culture in which it was set if he or she is to form a thorough understanding of the text.

Exercise

Look up the entomology (history) for each of the following words:

1. boycott

2. laconic

3. chauvinism

4. maverick

5. cynic

6. tantalize

7. Darwinism

8. Vandal

9. Machiavellian

10. Utopian

How Context Clues Improve Reading Speed

Most students do not realize that their reading speed may have contributed to their being in a foundational reading class. If you read too slowly, your comprehension will be adversely affected. In other words, you will have trouble concentrating and understanding what you read. College students' average reading speed is approximately 250 to 300 words per minute (wpm) with approximately 70 percent comprehension on nontechnical material. Of course, your reading speed will vary depending on the material you are reading. If you are reading textbook material, your reading speed may decrease, whereas if you are reading for pleasure, it may increase.

Context clues can help students increase their reading speed. This workbook has exercises designed to help you recognize and utilize context clues. It is important to note that when reading any piece of material, you should not look up words on the first reading. Instead, see if you can figure out unknown words by their context. If upon the second or third reading, you still cannot understand the material, then look up the unknown word.

Following are examples of how context clues work:

- *Example Context Clue*: Gives an example of the word in the material which tells you what the word means.

  Ted suffers from hypertension, which is a disease that increases a person's blood pressure.

  There is no need to look up the word hypertension because the sentence explains what hypertension is. Also, note that "or" may be a signal word that the meaning of the word will follow.

- *Restatement Context Clue*: *Restates what the word is.*

  Ted suffers from hypertension (high blood pressure).

- *Antonyms*: *Indicates the definition of a word by giving an opposite meaning.*

  My brother is always optimistic, unlike my sister who only sees the dark side of life and is a born pessimist.

- *Synonyms*: *Indicates the definition of a word by giving a word with the same meaning.*

  Ted took small items from work; he has always been noted for pilfering.

- _Punctuation Clues_: *Punctuation can also give clues that an explanation of a word is being revealed. Pay close attention to dashes, parenthesis, brackets, colons, and commas.*

In each exercise in this workbook, you will be asked to use the correct word in context and to underline the context clue. By becoming proficient or good at recognizing context clues, you will increase your reading speed, which will help you immensely in your college studies.

Context Clues Exercise:

- *Look up the meaning of the following words, then fill in the blank with the correct word from the above word bank and underline the context clue.*

boycott	chauvinism	cynic	Darwinism	Machiavellian
laconic	maverick	tantalize	vandal	utopian

Context clues using Antonyms and Synonyms

Antonyms: Select the word with the opposite meaning and write it in the blank

_____1. looks at everyone's point of view, open minded
_____2. speaks at length, wordy
_____3. benevolent, open and candid, thinks of others
_____4. disruptive society, chaos, disreputable government
_____5. not rash or impetuous, thinks through things carefully.

Synonyms: Select the word that has the same meaning and write it in the blank.

_____1. negative views, pessimistic
_____2. refusing to deal with another in order to punish or coerce
_____3. survival of the fittest, selective process of nature
_____4. tease, torment playfully
_____5. to tear down, destroys property, especially what is beautiful or valuable

Use the context clues in the following sentences to choose the best meaning:

1. My husband became irritated with the movie because it was set in the 1960's era, and the car the star was driving was from the 1970's. I did not notice this *anachronistic* detail; however, my husband's hobby is building car from that time period.

Anachronistic means:

a) silly   b) unnecessary   c) bold   d) out-of-date

2. If you allow that type of behavior to go on in front of your children, you are ***sanctioning*** it as being appropriate, and it is not.

Sanctioning means:

a) disapproval   b) approving   c) complete   d) interesting

Context Clues Exercise Continued:

- **Fill in the blank with the correct word from the above word bank and underline the context clue.**

boycott	chauvinism	cynic	Darwinism	Machiavellian
laconic	maverick	tantalize	vandal	utopian

1. Being a nonconformist did not serve Jim well in the military since being labeled as a
_____ hurt his chances of promotion.

2. George was noted for being brief when he spoke, and his _____ way of speaking actually made him more interesting to talk to.

3. Shakespeare's Richard III is a perfect example of a _____ .
However, some historians believe that Shakespeare portrayed him in as a crafty deceitful king to please Queen Elizabeth whose ancestors had disposed King Richard.

4. _____ states that nature permits species to survive according to how well they adapt to their environment.

5. My husband teased me about my birthday present for months; therefore, I decided that I would _____ him for his birthday also.

6. Ted was a _____. His extremely fanatical views made everyone in the meeting uncomfortable.

7. The word _____ comes from a German tribe who ravaged Gaul, Spain, and sacked Rome in A.D. 455.

8. A _____ society refers to a perfect and idolized community where everyone lives in peace and harmony. Sir Thomas More, an English statesman and scholar of King Henry VIII's court, wrote a book which used this word as its title. Ironically, he was beheaded by King Henry VIII for refusing to acknowledge the king as the head of the English Church.

9. Nicolas Chauvin was noted for being an extremist and a braggart regarding his super loyalty to Napoleon and France. We now use the word _____ to describe anyone who holds a biased and zealous devotion to any group or idea.

10. The word _____ originated from Captain Charles Boycott who was rebuffed by the Irish Land League in 1880 because he refused to work with them to reduce land rents. In 1955, Martin Luther King Jr. led a _____ called the Montgomery Bus _____ to oppose the arrest of Rosa Parks, who had been arrested for not giving up her seat to a white person. This was a major event of the civil rights movement.

Word Analysis

Sentences are made up of words just as words are made up of word elements or parts. Studying and memorizing word parts can help you learn vocabulary more easily and quickly. It can also help you increase your reading speed by helping you recognize the meaning of a word when it is used in the context of a sentence. Many words are divided into the following three parts: roots, prefixes, and suffixes.

Since English is a living language, it grows continually. Borrowing from other languages is one way that we constantly add to the vast number of English words. Another way that words are created is by combining word elements, such as roots, prefixes, and suffixes, which cannot stand alone.

Word Root: contains the core meaning of the word
Prefix: is always placed at the beginning of a word to change its meaning.
Suffix: is always placed at the end of a word to change its meaning.

Latin Roots, Prefixes, and Suffixes' History

Latin was the language spoken by the ancient Romans. As the Romans conquered most of Europe, the Latin language spread throughout the region. Over time, the Latin spoken in different areas developed into separate languages, including Italian, French, Spanish, and Portuguese. These languages are considered "sisters," as they all descended from Latin, their "mother" language.

In 1066 England was conquered by William, duke of Normandy, which is in northern France. For several hundred years after the Norman invasion, French was the language of court and polite society in England. It was during this period that many French words were borrowed into English. Linguists estimate that some 60% of our common everyday vocabulary today comes from French; therefore, many Latin words came into English indirectly through French.

However, many Latin words came into English directly too. Monks from Rome brought religious vocabulary as well as Christianity to England beginning in the 6th century. From the Middle Ages onward many scientific, scholarly, and legal terms were borrowed from Latin.

During the 17th and 18th centuries, dictionary writers and grammarians generally felt that English was an imperfect language whereas Latin was perfect. In order to improve the language, they deliberately made up English words from Latin words. For example, fraternity, from Latin fraternitas, was thought to be better than the native English word brotherhood.

Understanding How Word Parts Work:

By breaking down a word into parts and then recognizing what each part means, you will increase your vocabulary and also increase your reading speed.

Examples

Inspector:
Root: (Foundation of a word)   -spect-   "look"
Prefix: (Found at the beginning of a word)   in-   "into"
Suffix: (Found at the end of a word)   -or   "one who"

Soliloquy
Root: -loqu-   "to talk"
Prefix: sol-   "alone"
Suffix: -y   "state or character of"

Word Parts Exercise

Refer to your dictionary or thesaurus and write down words that use the following word part on the blank provided.

-itis	*inflammation or infection*
-meter	*a measurement*
-kine	*movement, moving*
-osis / -otic	*abnormal condition, disease*
-mycin	*derived from a fungus*
-jugal	*to yoke, join together*
-graph	*drawing, writing*
-fer	*bearer, producer, carry*
-emia	*blood disease*

Vocabulary Workbook Exercises

Courtesy of The Kobal Collection. Copyright © 20th Century Fox Film Corp.

(Young Frankenstein)

Unchaining Our Thoughts By
Putting It All Together

- **Vocabulary Worksheets:** The following vocabulary worksheets cover confusing words, words that are listed on the study guide for the SAT, literary terms, and name derivatives, which emphasize etymology, and in each of these worksheets, we will practice learning word parts, parts of speech, and using words in context.
- In the back of the booklet, there are supplemental lists of Latin and Greek derivatives (word parts), additional lists of confusing words, power verbs, and a list of conjunctive adverbs, prepositions, and coordinating conjunctions, power verbs.

Courtesy of the Everett Collection. Copyright ©20th Century Fox Film Corp.

- A supplemental list of additional SAT words is also located in the back of the booklet. If there are words on this list you do not know, you should take the time to learn them since these words are given on a college-level entrance examine.
- If you have a deficiency in grammar, you may reference the website listed in the supplemental section. They are geared more toward ESL students; however, since you may have only been exposed to your own dialect, learning and understanding standardized English may be similar to learning a foreign language since you must first translate the standardized English through the dialect that you have used and heard all your life. *Even when using your own dialect, you need to break yourself from using incorrect grammar. After all, it's your language. Get to know her.*

- By using the techniques outlined in this workbook, you will learn how to effectively master vocabulary, which will enable you not only to have a successful college career but also a more successful life — and to develop "a more sophisticated way of expressing [yourself]."

Courtesy of Mary Evans/Ronald Grant/Everett Collection.

Gene Wilder as Dr. Frankenstein and Peter Boyle as The Monster

Vocabulary Worksheet One
Power Verbs

Substituting power verbs for weak verbs will turn a boring essay into a more interesting one. Power verbs convey more meaning and catch the reader's attention.

Exercise One: Dictionary Skills

- *Look up the following words and write down the first definition, the word's phonetic spelling, its part of speech, and etymology. You also need to write a sentence using each word.*

advocated	designated	disseminated ✓	resolved ✓	diversified ✓
razed ✓	simulated ✓	elicited ✓	solidified ✓	improvised ✓

Exercise Two: Using Words in Context

- *Fill in the blank with the correct word from the above word bank and underline the context clue.*

1. He made an earnest decision to quit smoking. Although he had _____ to quit many times before, this time he had more motivation since his new girlfriend was allergic to cigarette smoke.

2. The politician _____ higher teacher salaries. Although he had recommended it publicly and promoted it in every campaign speech, the teachers were still dubious that he would actually follow through with his promise if he were elected.

3. The hospital _____ a crisis situation to help train their emergency personal. Since the scene they created was so lifelike, it helped the employees when an actual emergency arose.

4. The attorney _____ a response from the witness, even though he did not want to answer the question. However, the fact that the attorney had to draw the answer out of the witness helped prove his point.

5. The speaker _____ his speech since he did not have time to prepare before the event.

6. The committee _____ the company park for the annual barbeque. They specified that particular spot because the employees' families will be attending the event.

7. They _____ the water tower yesterday. It had been standing since the 1950s. It was sad to see the landmark demolished.

8. The students _____ the information about the upcoming play by posting bulletins. They also broadcast it on the local radio station.

9. He _____ his stocks. He wanted a portfolio which contained different types of investments.

10. The first section of concrete _____ quickly; however, the second section did not become solid until the next day.

Exercise Three: Word Parts

- ***Refer to your dictionary or thesaurus and write down words that use the following word parts.***

ann, enn	*year*
cred. credit	*believe, trust*
fid	*faith, trust*
greg	*flock*
litera	*letter*
man	*hand*
mater, matr, metr	*mother*
mor, mort	*death*
ped	*foot*
pon, posit	*place*

Exercise Four: Context clues using *Antonyms* and *Synonyms*

Antonyms: *Select the word with the opposite meaning*

_____ 1. planned, rehearsed, thought out, permanent
_____ 2. liquefy, dissolve, melt, thaw
_____ 3. ambiguous, changeable, contingent, doubtful, hazy

30

_____ 4. actual, original, real, bona fide, genuine
_____ 5. build, construct, assemble, erect

Synonyms: *Select the word with the same meaning*

_____ 1. recommend publicly, favor, support, promote, endorse
_____ 2. to scatter, spread widely, sowing seed, broadcast, disperse
_____ 3. indicate, to mark or point out, specify
_____ 4. vary, change, expand, rotate, different types
_____ 5. bring out, deduce, derive, discover, evoke, wring out

Exercise Five: *In the following sentences, substitute the verb or verb phrase in the sentence with one of the power verbs from this week's vocabulary.*

_____ 1. I had *to draw out* the information from him slowly.
_____ 2. I *supported* him for the position.
_____ 3. I *settled* the dispute with my friend.
_____ 4. I *varied* my plans to include buying additional property.
_____ 5. They *tore down* the school house where the six Amish school girls were murdered.

Exercise Six: Parts of Speech

- *Determine the part of speech (noun, verb, adjective, or adverb) of the italicized word in each sentence.*

_____ 1. The *simulative* fire drill imitated a real one.
_____ 2. His *resolvedly* opposed the bill.
_____ 3. The *dissemination* of the data was alarming since it was top secret information.
_____ 4. The ingredients were *solidifiable.*
_____ 5. The *solidification* of the mixture made it easier to handle.

Vocabulary Worksheet Two
Confusing Words

One of the most exasperating aspects of the English language is its vast number of confusing words. These words sound alike but have entirely different meanings and spellings. As college students who want to achieve a higher level of academic language, it is imperative that you use the "correct word." In the immortal words of Mark Twain in a letter that he wrote to George Bainton in 1888, "The difference between the almost right word & the right word is really a large matter—it's the difference between the lightning bug and the lightning."

Exercise One: Dictionary Skills
- *Look up the following words and write down on a separate sheet of paper each word's phonetic spelling, its part of speech, the definition, and etymology. You also need to write a sentence using the word.*

complement/compliment	number/amount	ladder/later/latter
foreword/forward	illusion/allusion	advise/advice
continuously/continually	uninterested/disinterested	adapt/adopt
capitol/capital	decent/descent	desert/dessert
break/brake	infer/imply	let/leave
everybody/every body	its/it's	except/accept
instance/instants	affect/effect	dual/duel

Exercise Two: Using Words in Context
- *Fill in the blank with the correct word from the above word bank. If there is a context clue in the sentence, underline it.*

1. The _____ of Arkansas is Little Rock.
2. A bicycle has _____ wheels. Children usually find trying to keep a bike upright with only two wheels is much harder than riding their tricycles.
3. Those black shoes _____ your black and white dress so well. It gives it a complete look.
4. Although her boyfriend did not think she was dressed appropriately, she felt that her dress was _____ and wore it anyway.
5. _____ had a different point of view about the project. Since there were so many individual opinions, no decision was made.
6. Getting together _____ this afternoon would be better for me because I have an appointment this morning. I know we're meeting after the usual time, but it would help me out today.
7. I counted twenty chairs in the auditorium; however, the actual _____ we need is twenty-one. Jan needs to bring in another chair from the storage room.
8. If you take the Orient Express, you can _____ from Istanbul, Turkey, and arrive in Paris. If you depart at an 8:00 AM instead of 1:00 PM, you can avoid arriving late at night.

9. Did you _____ that the plan won't work? If that is what you are hinting, then you need to state it clearly and offer an alternate solution.

10. Shakespeare's poem "My Mistress Eyes" is a humorous poem. _____ sarcastic tone is Shakespeare's attempt to satirize romantic poetry.

11. I _____ from your comment that you are interested in the overseas job. However, I could have drawn an incorrect conclusion.

12. _____ after the alarm sounded, all the students evacuated the building. Leaving the building within moments after the alarm sounded saved many lives because the tornado made a direct hit on the building they were in.

13. It looked as if the magician disappeared into thin air; however, it was just an _____ because he was actually standing just behind the curtain.

14. For _____, the movie *Apocalypse Now* is based on Joseph Conrad's book *Heart of Darkness*. The movie is a good example of how the overall theme and details of a book can be telescoped and adapted for movies.

15. _____ not important that the project is finished today.

16. It was hard to _____ my father's advice; however, I had to finally agree that he was correct.

17. We must keep pushing _____ because if we do not keep marching toward the fighting, we may lose the battle.

18. Since I am short, I always have to have a _____ to reach items that are out of my reach. The one I have helps me climb high enough to even dust my ceiling fans.

19. I could _____ easier to the culture if the food wasn't so different; however, I'm sure I will adjust to it in time.

20. The choir leader praised my voice. His _____ boosted my confidence.

21. I am _____ losing my keys. Time and time again, I leave them in silly places like my closet.

22. _____ agreed that the plan would work. Of course, the collective effort of the club will be needed to make it succeed.

23. The _____ is hot, arid, and dry.

24. Doctors initially did not realize the hazardous _____ of cigarette smoking on a person's health; therefore, smoking was accepted and even glamorized. However, cigarette smoking did not seem as glamorous when the medical field began to realize the results of smoking and finally linked it to lung cancer. In 1966, it became law that all cigarette packages display a label, warning the public that cigarette smoking could be hazardous to their health.

25. Is the Jackson family going to _____ a child from South America? This will not be the first time that they have taken children into their family.

26. _____ for two of the members, everyone is going on the trip to Asia. Even excluding those two, however, we still have enough members to justify the cost of the trip.

27. Until modern times, it was not uncommon for gentlemen to settle their disputes or fights by challenging each other to a _____, which was usually fought at sunrise.

28. The _____ of the book was torn out.

29. I asked my friend Sara for _____. Her opinions are always valuable.

30. The speaker spoke _____ for three hours. Since he continued lecturing without stopping, the dinner that followed his speech was delayed.
31. The _____ building is the most beautiful government building in the state. The state legislature is pleased with the remodeling.
32. I asked you not to _____ my favorite bowl. You've shattered it all over the floor.
33. The referee was always impartial when observing the football games. Although he loved the game itself, his _____ in the outcome made him a good referee.
34. There is no way to count to the _____ of sand in the desert.
35. The _____ we had last night at the end of our meal was deliciously sweet and went well with coffee.
36. The _____ on the car failed, and my mother ran into the back of a police car. The policeman gave her a ticket since it was a mechanical failure that she could have prevented.
37. She dropped an _____ at the party to the fact that her uncle was famous. However, her hints were lost on the group since they had never heard of him.
38. I would _____ you not to buy that stock. My stockbroker counseled me on how to invest in the stock market and cautioned me against buying that particular one.
39. Chief Dan George was of Cherokee Indian _____. He tried to hand down many of the legends and traditions of the Cherokee Nation's to future generations.
40. Your continual tardiness is going to _____ your grades. It could even influence your future if you do not learn how to be punctual.
41. I had an option of three different insurance plans, and I chose the _____.
42. You must not _____ your thoughts wander during the professor's lecture. If you allow yourself to become distracted, you will not hear valuable information.
43. Some students have no interest in reading; therefore, they are _____ in literature.

Exercise Three: Word Parts

- *Refer to your dictionary or thesaurus and write down words that use the following word part on the blank provided.*

-duc-	to lead, bring, take
-pend-	to hang
-port-	to carry
-vert-	to turn
-ject-	to throw
-scrib- / -script-	to write
pel	to drive

dict	to say
gress	to walk
tract	to pull, drag, draw

Exercise Four: Parts of Speech

- *Determine the part of speech (noun, verb, adjective, or adverb) of the italicized word in each of the following sentences.*

_____1. Ted *complimented* my singing.
_____2. The *foreword* of the book is torn.
_____3. James *adopted* a child from China.
_____4. The cowboys fought a *duel* at sunrise.
_____5. It rained *continuously* for three days.

Exercise Five: Matching – *Word Parts*

____1. tract
____2. duc
____3. gress
____4. pend
____5. ject
____6. port
____7. vert
____8. scrib, script
____9. pel
___10. dict

a. to hang
b. to write
c. to lead, bring, take
d. to walk
e. to carry
f. to turn
g. to throw
h. to drive
i. to say
j. to pull, drag, draw

Vocabulary Worksheet Three
(SAT Words)

Exercise One:

- *Look up the following words and write down on a separate sheet of paper the word's definition, its part of speech, and etymology. You also need to write a sentence using each word.*

compulsive	*deprive*	*deviant*	*plausible*	*prevalent*
denigrate	*noxious*	*enigma*	*perilous*	*ramification*

Exercise Two: Using Words in Context

- *Fill in the blank with the correct word from the above word bank and underline the context clue.*

1. Widespread cases of flu have been a problem this year. Although the flu is _____ this time of the year, the severity of these cases is affecting people's jobs.
2. The coach did not have to belittle Ted so severely in front of his team. To _____ a player in such a way is not helpful but is instead destructive to a person's self esteem.
3. His behavior fell far below even the social norm for prison. His fellow prisoners thought he was a _____.
4. Cleaning products are poisonous if swallowed. It is a good idea to keep all _____ cleaners safely away from children.
5. Karen had an obsessive need for orderliness and cleanliness. Her _____ behavior made it hard for her to relax.
6. Sonya's mother withheld her allowance for two weeks because her grades had fallen so drastically. Her mother also told her that if her grades did not improve that she would _____ her of her allowance again, only this time it would be for a longer period.
7. The consequence of your being late for work every day this week is going to be severe; in fact, the _____ could result in your losing your job.
8. I thought Sofia's excuse was totally reasonable. However, her professor did not think that it was a _____ excuse.
9. Riding the rapids down the river on a raft is extremely dangerous. However, the canoeist was determined to go through with this _____ feat.
10. Mona Lisa's smile has always mystified art critics. It will probably always remain an _____.

Exercise Three: Word Parts

- *Refer to your dictionary or thesaurus and write down words that use the following word part on the blank provided.*

Word Part	Meaning
aster	star
bio	life
crypt	hidden
demos	people
derm	skin
homo	same
log	speak
miss, mit	send
gener	bring forth
organ	system

Exercise Four: Context clues using *Antonyms* and *Synonyms*

Antonyms: *Select the word with the opposite meaning.*

_____1. rare, hard to find, infrequent, not pervasive
_____2. praise, respectful, compliment
_____3. safe, secure, nonhazardous, not risky
_____4. normal or standard behavior, typical, accepts appropriate social standards
_____5. relaxed, not stressed, patient, not obsessed with details

Synonyms: *Select the word with the same meaning.*

_____ 1. remove, deny, withhold
_____ 2. puzzle, mystery, riddle, secret
_____ 3. believable, reasonable, probably, credible
_____ 4. harmful, poisonous, lethal, toxic, evil
_____ 5. result, consequence, outcome, aftermath

Exercise Five: Parts of Speech
- *Determine the part of speech (noun, verb, adjective, or adverb) of the italicized word in each sentence.*

_____ 1. The *deviant* was put in jail for fifteen years.
_____ 2. The *deviant* behavior of pedophiles defies explanation.
_____ 3. I have *deviated* from my original plan.
_____ 4. The *perilously* long journey took four months.
_____ 5. The *ramification* of his sudden wealth caught him quite off guard.

- *Determine what part of speech (noun, verb, adjective, or adverb) of the italicized word in each sentence by looking at its suffix.*

_____ 1. compulsion
_____ 2. compulsively
_____ 3. denigrated
_____ 4. denigration
_____ 5. denigrative

Use the correct form of the italicized word in the following sentence:
Compulsive:
1. His _____ to complete the job was admirable.
2. John acted _____ when he gambled away his entire check.

Denigrate:
3. The _____ way he spoke to his wife was inexcusable.
4. The _____ he felt was overwhelming.
5. He _____ his family name by his immoral acts.

Exercise Six: Matching:

1. ___ prevalent   a) obsessed
2. ___ enigma   b) below standard
3. ___ compulsive   c) widespread
4. ___ deprive   d) poisonous
5. ___ noxious   e) dangerous
6. ___ ramification   f) criticize harshly
7. ___ deviant   g) consequence
8. ___ denigrate   i) withhold
9. ___ plausible   j) mystery
10. ___ perilous   k) reasonable

Vocabulary Worksheet Four
(SAT Words)

Exercise One: Dictionary Skills
- *Look up the following words and write down the word's phonetic spelling, its part of speech, the definition, and etymology. You also need to write a sentence using each word.*

assimilate	*attainment*	*heritage*	*indigenous*	*whereas*
influx	*median*	*multilingual*	*regardless*	*surpass*

Exercise Two: Using Words in Context
- *Fill in the blank with the correct word from the above word bank and underline the context clue.*

1. John always seems to blend in wherever he lives. He is extremely well educated and personable, which helps him _____ into his environment easier.
2. _____ of the weather, I plan to attend the conference. Therefore, in spite of the snow storm, you can count on me to be there.
3. Since alligators were once native to Arkansas, the Arkansas Game and Fish Commission decided to relocate the species into the state again. However, many people felt that even if they were _____ to Arkansas, there may have been a good reason why we eliminated them from the eco-system in the first place.
4. Jacob is a tall man with dark hair, _____ his brother Jack is short with blond hair. Although their appearances are contrary to each other, they both have easy going personalities.
5. The _____ corporate tax is lower in the south than the average or middle corporate tax of states in the north.
6. The impressive _____ of his multi-billion dollar estate was credited to his achievements in knowing how to invest wisely in the stock market.
7. The contribution to the hospital will _____ what we originally estimated. In fact, it will go beyond what we thought would be contributed over a two-year period.
8. The _____ of people attending the baseball game was exciting. However, their mass arrival was not overwhelming due to good planning.
9. Many companies must have _____ personnel. The need to know several languages has created a new job market for students graduating with a degree in foreign language.
10. Jim has an excellent _____. His inheritance not only included wealth but a prestigious family name.

Exercise Three: *Application: Fill in the blank using words from this week's vocabulary. Underline the context clue.*

Native Americans, those people (1) _____ to the Americas, have a proud ancestry, and their (2) _____ deserves serious reflection. (3) _____ of few appearances in print and film and in spite of the effect disease and poverty have had on Native Americans, they are, nevertheless, the oldest minority and currently have a population of two million. Many are (4) _____, speaking several languages from many tribes, as well as speaking English. Unfortunately their history has been filled with discrimination and exploitation since the mass arrival of Europeans in the 17th century. The (5) _____ of Europeans had a drastically negative effect on the Indian nations. Consequently some Native Americans remain isolated. Others, however, have left the reservation and have learned to (6) _____ or blend in with those outside the tribe. They have become well known in many areas. For example, the words of Black Hawk and Black Elk are studied today, in addition to the literature of Scott Momaday. Likewise, an industry promoting their art and music has 7)_____ original expectations and has gone beyond the profits they expected to make.

Some Native Americans are experiencing progress, 8) _____ many more continue to suffer educationally and economically. This contrast is most obvious in the (9)_____ or average income, which in many cases, remains below the poverty level, and the (10)_____ of a better life seems out of reach of what they can realistically achieve. Yet, it is not impossible if we remember the words of Lone Man (Isna-la-wica) Teton Sioux, who said, "I have seen that in any great undertaking, it is not enough for a man to depend simply upon himself." Thus, the struggle of one becomes the struggle of many.

Exercise Four: Word Parts

- *Refer to your dictionary or thesaurus and write down words that use the following Latin Root on the blank provided.*

alter-	change
spec-	look, watch
aqua-	water
aster, astro-	star
aud-	hear
bene-	good

40

pro-	forward/on behalf of
cap-	head
sub-	under/below
loc	place

Exercise Five: *Parts of Speech*

- *Determine what part of speech (noun, verb, adjective, or adverb) of the italicized word in each sentence.*

_____ 1. You will *assimilate* into college better if you join school-sponsored organizations and form study groups.
_____ 2. The *median* of the highway needs to be repaired.
_____ 3. *Multilingual* employees are in high demand in today's work force.
_____ 4. The *influx* of illegal aliens into our country is causing concern.
_____ 5. The *heritage* of native tribes is in danger of disappearing.

Exercise Six: *Use the correct form of the word in the blank and indicate its part of speech:*

1. assimilate / assimilation

_____ The _____ of new employees into the company will be difficult because they are so untrained.

2. surpass / surpassing

_____ Gloria was of _____ beauty.

3. attainment / attainable

_____ The goal was _____.

Vocabulary Worksheet Five
(SAT Words)

Exercise One: Dictionary Skills
- *Look up the following words and write down each word's phonetic spelling, its part of speech, the definition, and the etymology. You also need to write a sentence using each word.*

analytical	*boon*	*tangible*	*plethora*	*methodical*
reprehensible	*comparable*	*defy*	*beneficiary*	*rescind*

Exercise Two: Using Words in Context
- *Fill in the blank with the correct word from the above word bank and underline the context clue.*

1. Anthony's behavior toward his father was shameful. Although it made him angry, his sister told him that his conduct was _____.
2. Jeff's ideas for the next year's budget were _____ to his boss'; therefore, since their ideas were equivalent, Jeff's plan was accepted.
3. In Beouwulf, King Hrothgar, gives _____ to his warriors who have performed bravely. These blessings or gifts are made from gold.
4. The professor has an _____ style of teaching, and the students appreciate the way he breaks down the information into parts and discusses each segment thoroughly.
5. The excess of applicants was good because it provided a wide selection of prospective employees; however, the _____ of resumes also caused confusion among the hiring committee since there were so many applicants from which to choose.
6. Faye is _____ in everything she does. Her orderly manner is nerve racking to people because she is always pointing how they could do the job better.
7. James was the sole _____ of his father's will. He will receive all the benefits of his entire estate.
8. The witness retracted his statement; therefore, since the only witness had _____ his previous accusation, the defendant was exonerated.
9. A one-year old is cute when they _____ their parents; however, when a teenager challenges his or her parents, it is no longer humorous.
10. The scientist has to provide concrete evidence to support his idea. In fact, scientist should always have to provide _____ research to back up their theories.

Exercise Three: *Name of the part of speech (Noun, Adjective, Adverb, or Verb) for the underlined word in the following sentences:*

1. _____ An *analytical* approach is required for scientific research.
2. _____ The $5,000 was a *boon* I didn't expect.
3. _____ I wonder if he will *defy* his boss.

42

4. _____ I cannot *rescind* my statement; I will lose my credibility.
5. _____ The two plans are *comparable*.
6. _____ The professor's ideas on research are *analytically* sound
7. _____ His attitude was *reprehensible*.
8. _____ The Game and Fish Commission's report stated that there was a *plethora* of deer this hunting season.
9. _____ He *defyingly* stood his ground against the oncoming army.
10. _____ The *boonless* victory was disappointing.

Exercise Four: *Context clues using Antonyms and Synonyms*

Antonyms: *Select the word with the opposite meaning and write it in the blank.*
1. _____:disinherited, disown, deprive, disaffiliate, exclude
2. _____:imaginary, not real, untouchable
3. _____:careless, chaotic, disorganized, inaccurate
4. _____:meager amount, deficient, few
5. _____:comply, obey, surrender, yield

Synonyms: *Select the word that has the same meaning and write it in the blank.*

1. _____:detailed, perceptive, precise, thorough
2. _____:gift, blessing, favor, good fortune
3. _____:equal, equivalent, proportionate, commensurable
4. _____:shameful, extremely bad, heinous, base, condemnable
5. _____:retract, take back, nullify, repeal, abolish

Exercise Five: *Prefixes/Suffixes*

Prefix	Definition	(From Vocabulary) Example	Additional Example	Part of Speech
ana-	upward, throughout	analytical	_____	_____
com-	with, together	comparable	_____	_____
con-	against, opposition *also variant of com-* *with, together	conversely	_____	_____
de-	down, from, away	defy	_____	_____

Suffix	Definition	(From Vocabulary) Example	Additional Example	Part of Speech
-able	able to	comparable	_____	_____
-cal	like, resembling	methodical	_____	_____
-fy	make	defy	_____	_____
-ish	resembling	diminish	_____	_____
-ly	in a certain manner	conversely	_____	_____
-ary	connected with	beneficiary	_____	_____

Exercise Six: *Additional Practice with Word Parts: Below a word is given, such as "contentious" and is then broken down. Try to figure out the meaning of the word by looking at what each word part means.*

1. ***Contentious***
- *con* means *against*
- *tent* means *to pay heed to*
- *ous* signifies that the word is an *adjective*

      Contentious means:
      a) quarrelsome   b) agreement   c) act   d) evidence

2. ***Concentrate***
- con – from Latin *com,* meaning *together*
- centrum – Latin word meaning *center*

      Concentrate *means:*
      a) to scatter   b) draw toward common center   c) to dilute

3. ***Anadromous*** means: (taken from Greek word anadromos)
- ana – means *up, upward*
- dromos – means *race*

      Anadromous means:
      a) migrating upstream at a specific time of the year to breed
      b) able to live without oxygen
      c) an interpretation of a word

Exercise Seven: Word Parts - *Matching*

1. ___ -ly	a) connected with
2. ___ -fy	b) down, from, away
3. ___ -de-	d) like, resembling
4. ___ -able	e) with, together
5. ___ com-	f) make
6. ___ ana-	g) against, opposition
7. ___ -cal-, -ish-	h) in a certain manner
8. ___ con-	i) upward, throughout
9. ___ -ary	j) able, to

*Number 8 has two answers.

Vocabulary Worksheet Six
(SAT Words)

Exercise One: Dictionary Skills

- *Look up the following words and write down each word's phonetic spelling, its part of speech, the definition, and etymology. You also need to write a sentence using the word.*

affable	*altruistic*	*ambidextrous*	*aromatic*
asinine	*candid*	*dogmatic*	*dubious*
eccentric	*impromptu*		

Exercise Two: Vocabulary: *Write the correct word in the blank:*

1. ____ **affable** (af'ah-bal) adj. The professor was an *affable* gentleman who always spoke when he saw his students.

   affable means:
   a. hostile   b. brilliant   c. dull   d. friendly

2. ____ **asinine** (as'ah nin') adj. The fan's *asinine* remark was totally unnecessary since the player hit a home run the next play.

   asinine means:
   a. flattering   b. playful   c. stupid   d. boasting

3. ____ **eccentric** (ik sen' trik) adj. The professor thought the student who came to class wearing a batman costume was *eccentric.*

   eccentric means:
   a. rude   b. defiant   c. smart   d. peculiar

4. ____ **altruistic** (al' troo is tik) adj. Mother Theresa was an extremely *altruistic* person. When she was awarded the Nobel Prize, she gave the money that would have been spent for the dinner to honor her to the poor.

   altruistic means:
   a. selfish   b. friendly   c. motherly   d. unselfish

5. ____ **candid** (kan did) adj.   It's important that you give me a *candid* answer so that I can make a clear decision.

   candid means:
   a. smart/intelligent   b. outspoken/frank   c. happy/cheerful

6. ____ **impromptu** (im promp' too) adj. Called on unexpectedly, the speaker gave a wonderful *impromptu* speech.

    Impromptu means:
    a. spur of the moment   b. with enthusiasm   d. nervous

7. ____ **ambidextrous** (am' bah dek' srahs) adj. The *ambidextrous* player was an asset to his basketball team.

    ambidextrous means:
    a. right handed   b. graceful   c. clumsy   d. use both hands equally

8. ____ **dogmatic** (dog mat' ik) adj. The dogmatic speaker spoke loudly and at length.

    dogmatic means:
    a. opinionated   b. kind   c. vague   d. needy

9. ____ **aromatic** (ar' nah mat' ik) adj. The bakery was *aromatic* and sold delicious bread.

    aromatic means:
    a. warm   b. loud   c. fragrant   d. distasteful

10. ____ **dubious** (doo bi ahs) adj. Although my husband promised that he truly needed a new sports car, I was *dubious.*

    dubious means:
    a. sound   b. logical   c. doubtful   d. believable

Exercise Three: *Vocabulary in Context. Fill in the blank with the correct word and underline the context clue:*

    Although the Vikings were the first to arrive in the Americas, Christopher Columbus (1451-1506) was a navigator and colonialist whose original plan was to try to find the western route to the Orient when he instead discovered the Americas. Since most people of his day did not believe his calculations that the Orient was a distance of 2,400 miles, they were
1)_____ that he could actually accomplish the trip and thought him
2)_____, thinking his ideas were peculiar. Although it is a mistake to believe that all people of the fifteen and sixteenth century stupidly believed the world was flat; nevertheless, some uneducated people still held the 3)_____ belief that the world was flat and that he and his crew would sail off the edge of the world. He was outspoken about his belief that he could reach the Orient, and monarchs Ferdinand II and Isabella I of Spain appreciated his
4)_____ argument that he could bring riches and spices to their country if they would finance his trip. Their 5)_____ or generous attitude toward financing him for his

adventure helped supply him with enough money so that he could accomplish his goal. He may possibly have been an 6)_____ person who spoke with a friendly confidence to his superiors, which would have benefited him immensely. The trip was not 7)_____ but was planned carefully. There were times when the seas were so stormy and the tempest raged so badly that the sailors not only had to use all their sailing skills but probably wished they were 8)_____ since deftly using both hands would have been a major asset to a sailor. When Columbus finally set sail, the sea must have smelled 9)_____ to him; its fragrance reminding him that he was actually on his way to the high seas and adventure. As fate would have it, he never realized at that time that he would become one of the most famous people in European history. Although he did not accomplish his original plan of reaching the Orient; nevertheless, his 10)_____ or opinionated beliefs lead him to the Americas.

Exercise Four: *Context clues using Antonyms and Synonyms*
Synonyms: Select the word that has the same meaning and write it in the blank
1. _____ friendly, easy to talk to, amiable
2. _____ stupid, silly, ass-like
3. _____ outspoken, unprejudiced, frank
4. _____ spontaneous, offhand, spur of the moment,
5. _____ unselfish, concerned for others

Antonyms: Select the letter of the word with the opposite meaning.
1. _____ trustworthy, believable, unquestionable
2. _____ reasonable listens to all opinions
3. _____ stinks, pungent, odor, smelly
4. _____ can use only right or left hand, cannot use both hands equally
5. _____ acts normal, well adjusted

Exercise Five: Parts of Speech: *Determine what part of speech the following word is:*
(Noun, Adjective, Adverb, or Verb)
1. _____ He behaved *asininely* toward his friend.
2. _____ His *affability* and positive attitude were refreshing.
3. _____ Jan's *altruism* resulted in her achieving a humanitarian aw

Exercise Six: Vocabulary - *Matching:*
1._____ impromptu
2._____ eccentric
3._____ asinine
4._____ affable
5._____ candid
6._____ altruistic
7._____ dubious
8._____ ambidextrous
9._____ dogmatic
10._____ aromatic

a. outspoken, frank, open
b. strongly opinioned
c. doubtful
d. fragrant
e. done on the spur or the moment
f. ability to use both hands equally
g. stupid, silly
h. generous
I. peculiar behavior
k. friendly

Exercise Seven: Word Parts:
- *Refer to your dictionary or thesaurus and write down words that use the following Latin root on the blank provided.*

the-	*god, spirit*
amphi-	*around, both sides*
-arch-	*chief, ruler, leader*
pyr-	*fire*
-phon-	*sound*
physi-	*nature*
anti-	*against*
pseudo-	*false*
tele	*far*
psych	*mind, spirit*

Exercise Eight: *Word Parts: Circle the letter for the correct word.*
1. tele = far
   phon = sound
      a) telephone   b) radio   c) CD   d) radio waves

Pick the correct definition of the following words:

2. **hierarchy**

    hier or hiero = sacred, holy
    arch   = chief, ruler, leader
    y   = condition, state, quality
    - a) a case or covering
    - b) one who has or pretends to have a superior learning or culture
    - c) a body of clergy (religious leaders) organized into successive ranks or rule

3. **monarchy**

    mon or mono = one
    arch   = chief, ruler, leader
    y   = condition, state, quality
    - a) the act of supplying
    - b) the act of practice of singing psalms
    - c) one ruler

4. **pseudonym**

    pseudo   = false
    nym or (French) nyme = name
    - a) a woman's married name
    - b) pertaining to the human mind
    - c) false name

Exercise Nine: *Word Parts - Matching*

1. ___ the		a) sound
2. ___ arch		b) chief, ruler, leader
3. ___ phon		c) nature
4. ___ physi		d) mind, spirit
5. ___ anti		e) far
6. ___ pyr		f) false
7. ___ pseudo		g) god
8. ___ tele		h) fire
9. ___ psych		i) around, on both sides
10.___ amphi		j) against

Vocabulary Worksheet Seven
(SAT Words)

Exercise One: Dictionary Skills
- *Look up the following words and write down each word's phonetic spelling, its part of speech, the definition, and etymology. You also need to write a sentence using the word.*

drudgery	contaminate	susceptible	idiosyncrasy	placid
blatant	congregate	unscrupulous	vivid	robust

Exercise Two: Using Words in Context
- *Fill in the blank with the correct word from the above word bank. If there is a context clue in the sentence, underline it.*

1. I dreaded going to work each morning since my job was tiresome, and after years of _____, I finally quit and found another job that was more interesting.
2. The brilliant hues of the Waterhouse painting were so lively. The paintings _____ colors were noted by all the art critics.
3. Since young children are so innocent, it makes them _____ to adult influence. Parents should guard them carefully since they are so vulnerable to being taken advantage of by deviate people.
4. If large companies continue to _____ our lakes, they will become polluted, tainted, and unusable to future generations.
5. Gather all the children into the hallway if you hear a fire alarm. They are supposed to _____ there before they are led safely outside.
6. The band noisily tuned up their instruments. Their _____ attempts to prepare for the concert was to no avail since they had not practiced and were not prepared.
7. A vigorous workout in the morning will wake you up and help you feel _____ for the entire day.
8. He had a peculiar habit of eating catsup and mustard on his eggs. This particular _____ made his wife ill to watch.
9. A person who lacks morals is said to be an _____ individual.
10. The baby was always noted for being calm and good natured. His parents appreciated his _____ personality, especially since he also sleep throughout the night.

Exercise Three: *Context clues using Antonyms and Synonyms*
Synonyms: Write the word in the blank that matches the closest.
1. _____ :brilliant, intense bright (as in color), lively
2. _____ :to make impure, taint, mix in something unclean or bad
3. _____ :a habit, mannerism, way of doing things that is peculiar to an individual
4. _____ :impressionable, open to influence
5. _____ :obvious, noisily, brazen, flagrant

Antonyms: Write the word in the blank that is the opposite in meaning:

1. _____ : upset, disturbed, easily made mad
2. _____ : moral, good character, honest
3. _____ : weak, not in good health, timid
4. _____ : enthusiastic, interesting, not boring
5. _____ : separate, not together

**Exercise Four*: Vocabulary in Context: Fill in the Blank with the correct word and underline the context clue:*

Although the job was tiresome and boring, the workers decided to face the 1)_____ of the job and clean up the lake since the tainted waters also threatened to 2)_____ the nearby streams where they lived. The lake's 3)_____ waters and the calm day helped make the job at least more pleasant. However, this did not last long before dark clouds began to 4)_____ on the horizon, and as they gathered and grew darker, the worker's noisy objections grew louder as they made their displeasure apparent to their employer. They 5)_____ objected to continuing their work because they felt that they would be 6)_____ not only becoming ill from working in the rain but would be vulnerable to a lightning strike. They also felt that the company who had polluted the lake should be responsible for cleaning it up since their 7)_____ and immoral behavior had made the lake unsafe. Their boss, however, was peculiar and felt that one should finish a job no matter what the weather conditions were. His 8)_____ was not appreciated by his employees. However, he was a man of vigorous energy, and his 9)_____ nature and willingness to work himself finally convinced his men to continue the job. Luckily, the storm passed, and the sky turned a 10)_____ blue once more, and its brilliance made the men's attitude more positive again.

Exercise Five: Word Parts
- *Refer to your dictionary or thesaurus and write down words that use the following Latin root on the blank provided.*

semi	*half, partly*
dia	*across, through*
mal, male	*bad, wrong*
omni	*all, everywhere*

51

re	again, back
circum	around
se	apart
inter	between, among
post	after
un	not

Exercise Six: Matching: Vocabulary

_____	1. unscrupulous	a) lively, brilliant
_____	2. drudgery	b) calm, good natured
_____	3. blatantly	c) vulnerable
_____	4. placid	d) polluted, tainted, unusable
_____	5. idiosyncrasy	e) gather
_____	6. contaminate	f) noisily, obviously
_____	7. robust	g) peculiar
_____	8. vivid	h) no or low morals
_____	9. susceptible	i) vigorous, strong, full flavored
_____	10. congregate	j) tiresome

Exercise Seven: Matching: Word Parts

_____	1. semi	a) all; everywhere
_____	2. dia	b) not
_____	3. mal, male	c) bad; wrong
_____	4. omni	d) apart
_____	5. re	e) after
_____	6. circum	f) across
_____	7. se	g) again; back
_____	8. inter	h) between; among
_____	9. post	i) around
_____	10. un	j) half; partly

Exercise Eight: *Practice with Word Parts*

androgynous:
- andro = man/male
- gyn = woman/female
- ous = adjective suffix

androgynous means:
   a) a male chauvinist   b) a feminist   c) having male and female characteristics in one

hypoglycemia:
- hypo = below, less, under
- glyc(o) = sweet, sugar
- mia

hypoglycemia means:
   a) a person who likes desserts   b) a person who doesn't like sugar
   c) abnormally low levels of sugar   d) a dessert that isn't sweet enough

abnormal:
- ab = away, off from, down
- normal = standard, typical

abnormal means:
   a) conformist   b) not normal or average   c) a typical person

Vocabulary Worksheet Eight
(SAT Words)

Exercise One: Dictionary Skills

- *Look up the following words and write down each word's phonetic spelling, its part of speech, the definition, and etymology. You also need to write a sentence using the word.*

aesthetic	degenerate	anachronistic	introspective	pungent
abbreviate	leniency	adulation	rampant	abstinence

Exercise Two: *Fill in the blank with the correct word and underline the context clue.*

1. The city's requirements for building standards have fallen well below what they were in the 1970s. In fact, their standards have become so _____ that many people are moving further out into the suburbs.
2. The unruly child ran _____ throughout the store while his mother yelled at him. One of the customers told the mother that she should restrain her child's wild behavior.
3. The _____ odor came from the trash bin. The sharp smell was caused from rotting vegetables that had been thrown in the bin without having been wrapped in plastic first.
4. He flattered the model excessively, and she found his _____ irritating.
5. I'll show you _____ this time if you promise not to do it again. However, I won't tolerate this type of behavior again.
6. If you _____ the state's name make sure to have the correct letters. The shortened form of Missouri is MO.
7. The _____1950s restaurant is popular, despite the fact that young people might think that it is out-of-date.
8. An alcoholic must practice _____. If a person who suffers from alcoholism does not practice total self-restraint, they will never conquer the disease.
9. James was a quiet _____ type person. He always examined his own mind and feelings before making a judgment.
10. Japanese art if well known for its _____ beauty. Its artistic appeal comes from its simplicity.

Exercise Three: *Context clues using Antonyms and Synonyms*

Synonym: *Select the word that has the same meaning and write it in the blank.*

_____ 1. frequently, without restraint, wildly, menacingly
_____ 2. decline, deteriorate, retrogress, worsen
_____ 3. self restraint, self denial
_____ 4. agreeable, tolerant, permissive, indulgent
_____ 5. excessive admiration, devotion, flatter, admire

Antonym: *Select the word(s) with the opposite meaning and write it in the blank.*

_____ 1. modern, current, new age

_____ 2. unappealing, lack of beauty, ugly

_____ 3. sweet smelling, aromatic, pleasantly sweet, mild

_____ 4. lengthen, write out fully, enlarge

_____ 5. insensitive, responds to only external events, not thoughtful

Exercise Four: Vocabulary in Context: Fill in the blank with the correct word and underline the context clue:

The fictional character Dracula is actually loosely based on an historic character named Vlad III, also known as Vlad the Impaler. Many Saxons, who lived in neighboring Transylvania, believed him to be a 1)_____, whose lack of humanity fell far below what most believe to be human. Some historians believe that he showed no 2)_____ for his enemies, and his intolerance led to the killing of political rivals, criminals, or anyone he deemed to be useless. He practiced no 3)_____ when it came to revenge, and his lack of self restraint, by some accounts, led to the impaling of 20,000 to 40,000 European civilians. However, some Romanians revered him as a defender of the Christian faith, and his menacing and 4)_____ killing of possibly 100,000 Muslim Turks made him a hero to many Christians. Some of the 5)_____ they showed him may have been given in hopes that flattery would gain his favor since he was such a formidable enemy. The victims were impaled on a stake and left to rot. The scent must have been 6)_____, and there was no beauty or 7)_____ appeal to the sight of thousands upon thousands of bodies decaying in the sun. Still, many Christian Romanians felt that since he was defending what they believed to be the true faith, his actions were justified; however, if one is more 8)_____ and examines the evidence thoughtfully, you will realize that it was merely the actions of a madman. In Bram Stoker's novel *Dracula,* he shortens and mostly ignores facts that surround the story of Dracula and 9)_____ the actual events that surround Count Vlad III, creating instead a creature that drinks the blood of his victims, instead of spilling their blood by impaling them on the battlefield, and is immortal. Although Dracula may seem out-of-date in our modern world, his (10)_____ blood-thirsty character has still reached a level of immortality through the character of Bram Stoker's *Dracula.*

Exercise Five: Word Parts

- *Refer to your dictionary or thesaurus and write down words that use the following Latin Root on the blank provided*

glycol	sugar, sweet
hydro	wet, water
mega	large, great

medius	middle
micro	small
mono	one
multi	many
neo	new
thermo	heat, warm
am, amat	love

Exercise Six: *Matching*

1. ___ hydro		a) heat, warm
2. ___ mega		b) wet, water
3. ___ thermo		c) great, large
4. ___ glyco		d) many
5. ___ medius		e) new
6. ___ multi		f) middle
7. ___ micro		g) sugar, sweet
8. ___ mono		h) one
9. ___ am, amat		i) small
10.___ neo		k) love

Vocabulary Worksheet Nine
(SAT Words)

Exercise One: Dictionary Skills
- *Look up the following words and write down the word's phonetic spelling, its part of speech, the definition, and etymology. You also need to write a sentence using the word.*

anonymous	*assiduous*	*benevolent*	*camaraderie*
censure	*collaborate*	*conformist*	*digression*
discredit	*empathy*		

Exercise Two: Using Words in Context
- *Fill in the blank with the correct word from the above word bank and underline the context clue.*

1. If we work together on this project, we should be able to finish it by tomorrow; however, if we don't _____, we may never finish it.
2. The professor often strayed from the point; however, at times, we learned more from his _____ than we did from the textbook.
3. The witness wanted to remain nameless. The police had warned him that if he didn't remain _____, his life might be in jeopardy.
4. Jane's father had passed away the year before, so she knew how Luke felt when his died. Because of her _____ toward him, they became life-long friends.
5. Men who have been in war together share a strong bond of brotherhood because they have had to trust each other in combat situations. This _____ among war veterans is common.
6. This type of behavior will _____ your family's name. If you continue to disgrace yourself, you will greatly disappoint your parents.
7. Jessica always follows the rules and customs, which irritates her sister Kaitlin who is not a _____.
8. Jim's _____ of Josie's performance made her cry. She felt that he had criticized her too harshly.
9. He is a most _____ young man, and his hard work will pay off for him when he gets his college degree
10. Martha is an extremely kind and friendly person, and her _____ attitude has won her the respect of all her neighbors.

Exercise Three: *Name of the part of speech (Noun, Adjective, Adverb, or Verb) for the underlined word in the following sentences:*

_____ 1. The prosecuting attorney *discredited* the witness.
_____ 2. The man was a *discredit* to his company.
_____ 3. The professor's *digression* from the point of his lecture was normal for him.

57

_____ 4. The *camaraderie* among the friends in the club was strong.
_____ 5. Larry's *benevolent* behavior made him popular.
_____ 6. Tim's boss *censured* him strongly for missing the deadline.
_____ 7. The *anonymous* note stated that the ransom will take place at
    midnight.
_____ 8. He was a *conformist.*
_____ 9. We must *collaborate* on this project.
_____ 10. I felt *empathy* for the young woman who had lost her dog.

Exercise Four: *Context clues using Antonyms and Synonyms*

Antonyms: Select the word with the opposite meaning and write it in the blank
_____ 1. well known, a person's name
_____ 2. rebel, individualistic, stand out in the crowd
_____ 3. focus, sticking to the subject
_____ 4. enemies, distrust
_____ 5. working independently, lack of cooperation

Synonyms: Select the word that has the same meaning and write it in the blank.
_____ 1. disparage, disgrace, tainted, undermine
_____ 2. hard working, diligent, tireless
_____ 3. understanding and entering into another's feelings
_____ 4. helpful, friendly, caring
_____ 5. criticize, disapproval, blame

Exercise Five: *Vocabulary in Context: Fill in the blank with the correct word and underline the context clue.*

The great humanitarian Mother Teresa was born August 26, 1910, and died September 5, 1997. She is noted for being one of the most 1)_____ people of our century, and her friendly and helpful ways helped save thousands of lives. She felt a trust among her friends within the Catholic Church, and this 2)_____ proved useful in her endeavors to help the masses of starving people who lived in her home town of Calcutta. Some may have called her a 3)_____ since she did follow the customs of her church closely; however, her devotion to her church have helped her achieve a greatness that has outlived her life, this being her great capacity to endure personal suffering while trying to help her fellow man. In 1948, she left the comfort and security of her convent to live among the poor. As a result, she experienced great hardship and began to share the feelings that the poor felt while struggling with poverty herself. Her 4)_____ helped her finally realize the actual horrors of stark poverty. She is quoted as saying, "Our Lord wants me to be a free nun covered with the poverty of the cross. Today I learned a good lesson. The poverty of the poor must be so hard for them. While looking for a home I walked and walked till my arms and legs ached. I thought how much they must ache in body and soul, looking for a home, food and health" (Byfield 125). Over the years, she successfully 5)_____ with foreign nations, and because she worked together well with them, she was able to raise millions of dollars in charity for the poor. Although she worked tirelessly for the poor, her 6)_____ efforts has, nevertheless, drawn criticism. Many critics have 7)_____ her for merely aiding the poor and not trying harder to eliminate the source of their poverty. Perhaps she did not stray from the original point of her mission; however, her lack of 8)_____ may have been what she felt that she was capable of doing, and to nameless thousands, her name means charity. These 9)_____ people revere her name. Many critics have also tried to 10)_____ her name because during her hardships, she at times felt doubtful, weary, and sad; however, to millions other, this attempt to disparage or disgrace her name did not work because they felt that overcoming doubts and frustrations simply attested to her strength of character and the fact that her love for mankind outweighed her own doubts and personal discomfort.

Exercise Six: Word Parts
- *Refer to your dictionary or thesaurus and write down words that use the following word parts on the blank provided.*

hydro	*water*

---

cau	*burn*

---

edem	*swell*

---

flex, flec	*bend*

---

flu, flux	*flow*

---

phobia	*fear*

---

scope	*examine*

---

topo	*place*

Exercise Seven: *Practice with Word Parts:*

topograph
- topo = place, region
- graph = a drawing or a diagram representing a system of connections or interrelations among two or more things by a number of distinctive dots, lines, bars, etc.

topograph means:
a) a place on top of a mountain   b) a region of the country

c) a detailed and precise description of a place or region

flexible
- flex = bend or bendable
- able = able to

flexible means:
a) to exercise   b) to bend something into shape   c) the ability of bend easily

hydrophobia
- hydro = water
- phobia = abnormal or illogical fear of something

hydrophobia means:
a) abnormal behavior   b) fear of storms   c) fear of water

Vocabulary Worksheet Ten
(SAT Words)

Exercise One: Dictionary Skills
- *Look up the following words and write down each word's phonetic spelling, its part of speech, the definition, and etymology. You also need to write a sentence using the word.*

emulate	enhance	ephemeral	extenuating	intrepid
haughty	hedonist	impetuous	impute	inevitable

Exercise Two: Using Words in Context
- *Fill in the blank with the correct word from the above word bank and underline the context clue.*

1. While attending college, Jim was always known as a pleasure seeker; however, his _____ attitude created problems when his partying interfered with his studies, and he eventually had to drop out of school.
2. Scotsman, William Wallace, was utterly fearless and won many battles against the Edward Longshanks, who was the brutal king who ruled England and terrorized Scotland; however, his _____ attitude toward battle eventually ended with his being drawn and quartered
3. Always follow the instructor's example. In fact, if you _____ what he is doing exactly, you will learn the sport much faster.
4. Since Sally and Ted lived in a small town, it made their running into each other after their breakup _____; however, since they had parted on good terms, it made the unavoidable much easier.
5. He is so arrogant. His _____ attitude is not winning him many friends.
6. The sunset was so alluring and serene in those fleeting moments right before it dropped beyond the verge. The effect of those _____ moments relaxed me for the entire evening.
7. You acted rashly when you bought the new car without checking with other car dealerships for better prices. Your _____ act has cost you around $5,000.
8. I don't want attribute too much praise onto one person. However, I can _____ top management skills for our success and most of the credit goes to Rob.
9. I don't mean to make light of the situation, but the project failed due to _____ circumstances that were beyond our control.
10. Her new hair style improved her overall appearance. It especially _____ her face.

Exercise Three: *Context clues using Antonyms and Synonyms*

Synonyms: Select the word that has the same meaning and write it in the blank.
1. _____ brief, fleeting, evanescent, transient, momentary
2. _____ follow, copy, imitate

61

3. _____proud, lordly, disdainful, contemptuous
4. _____rash, accidental, not by design, not planned
5. _____attribute, imply, something originating with a specific person

Antonyms: Select the word with the opposite meaning and write it in the blank
1. _____diminish, reduce, dull down
2. _____serious minded, thoughtful
3. _____overestimate, make more serious, overrate
4. _____timid, frightened easily, cowardly
5. _____avoidable, destined to occur, alterable

Exercise Four: Vocabulary in Context: Fill in the blank with the correct word and underline the context clue.

The Intrepid Warrior

It was unavoidable that William Wallace's would die tragically. His 1)_____ death was brought about by a Scotsman and Lord, William the Bruce, who betrayed him before a major battle. Wallace was fearless on the battlefield and fought valiantly against the armies of King Edward Longshanks, who was the tyrant who ruled England and terrorized Scotland. Wallace was totally fearless, and his 2)_____ attitude on the battlefield won battles, and although his methods may have seemed somewhat rash to some, his 3)_____ personality won battles and inspired his men. Although many excellent commanders die, leaving only a fleeting memory of their attainments, Wallace's legend was not 4)_____nor did he die in vain. William the Bruce realized his grave mistake and took it upon himself to embrace Wallace's ideology that men should be free. Bruce followed Wallace's example and 5)_____ him on the battlefield, which led to the freeing of Scotland from England. He also improved his own station in life and 6)_____ his title and land holdings. Although Wallace's men originally 7)_____ treachery to Bruce, they finally no longer attributed treachery to his name when he fought for them fearlessly, which diminished their original hatred of him for betraying Wallace because they felt he had been influenced by 8)_____ circumstances. Bruce proved to be an excellent commander and defeated the pleasure seeking King Edward II; Edward Longshank's 9)_____ son. Edward II was an ineffectual and weak leader, which was totally unlike his arrogant father whose 10) _____ attitude only added to the hatred that the men of Scotland felt for him.

Exercise Five: *Name of the part of speech (Noun, Adjective, Adverb, or Verb) for the underlined word in the following sentences:*

_____ 1. If you *emulate* his bad study habits, you will not do well in school either.
_____ 2. Joe's *hedonist* attitude worried his father.
_____ 3. The *inevitable* consequence of drinking and driving is usually death.
_____ 4. The *ephemeral* moments of life pass by quickly so savor them.
_____ 5. That was an *impetuous* act.

Exercise Six: *Word Parts*
- *Refer to your dictionary or thesaurus and write down words that use the following Latin Root on the blank provided.*

ante	*before*
co	*together*
de	*away*
quadr	*four*
quasi	*seemingly, not actually*
retro	*back*
ultra	*very, beyond*
path	*disease, feeling*
sequ, secut	*follow*
sign	*sign*

Vocabulary Worksheet Eleven
(SAT Words)

Exercise One: Dictionary Skills

- *Look up the following words and write down each word's phonetic spelling, its part of speech, the definition, and etymology. You also need to write a sentence using the word.*

alienate	*deft*	*loathe*	*proliferation*	*sundry*
congruence	*rebuttal*	*latent*	*lethargic*	*anomaly*

Exercise Two: Using Words in Context

- *Fill in the blank with the correct word from the above word bank and underline the context clue.*

1. The butcher shop sold various hams, selected beef, and lamb. The _____ items were all arranged in a refrigerated case, which made an attractive display.

2. There was a _____ among the congressman to pass the new bill; however, before an agreement was finally reached, the congressman had argued for days.

3. Ted's quiet nature made him an _____ in his family because they were extremely extraverted and thought his quietness odd.

4. Janie _____ all her friends when she was so rude at the party. She resented their hostile attitude toward her and would not admit that she had done anything wrong.

5. I felt _____ last week. In fact, I felt so sluggish and listless that I didn't even go to work.

6. He is such a skillful piano player. His hands are not only _____, but he also has extraordinarily long fingers.

7. The worldwide _____ of nuclear weapons is a major problem. The rapid spread of these destructive weapons affects everyone in the world.

8. The lawyer's _____ was quite impressive. His denial of his client's guilt was convincing.

9. James detests people who spread malicious gossip. He also _____ people who listen to the gossip.

10. The disease was dormant for ten years, and then the _____ cancer cells started to grow, and the patient has been given only two months to live.

Exercise Three: Context clues using Antonyms and Synonyms

Synonyms: Select the word that has the same meaning and write it in the blank.

1. _____   concealed, hidden, idle, sleeping, unripe
2. _____   able, adept, agile, skillful, skilled
3. _____   come between, estrange, separate, turn away
4. _____   dislike, abhor, hate, reject
5. _____   assorted, different types, many, several

Antonyms: Select the word with the opposite meaning and write it in the blank

1. _____ disagreement, discord, friction, strife
2. _____ acceptance, admission, approval, affirmation
3. _____ active, full of energy, robust
4. _____ decrease, shrinking, not growing
5. _____ average, conformity, sameness, the norm

Exercise Four: Name of the part of speech (Noun, Adjective, Adverb, or Verb) for the underlined word in the following sentences:

1. _____ He had a *latent* ability for playing the piano.
2. _____ The *rebuttal* helped the debating team win the debate.
3. _____ He was an *anomaly* among his friends because he did not drink.
4. _____ Jerry has *alienated* all of his friends with his behavior.
5. _____ I *loathe* spinach.

Exercise Five: **Word Parts**
- *Refer to your dictionary or thesaurus and write down words that use the following Latin Root on the blank provided.*

satis	enough of
prim(o)	first
some	body
super	above, on top of
ex	out of
ad	to, toward
terra	land
pater	father
frater	brother
genus	birth, offspring

Exercise 6: *Practice with Word Parts:*

satisfy

- satis = enough of
- fy = make

satisfy means:

a) to fulfill one's needs or desires   b) to be unhappy   c) to overrate something

export

- ex = out of
- port = carry

export means:

a) take out food   b) to send to another place   c) to go on a trip

Vocabulary Worksheet Twelve
(SAT Words)

Exercise One: Dictionary Skills
- *Look up the following words and write down the word's phonetic spelling, its part of speech, the definition, and etymology. You also need to write a sentence using the word.*

vicarious	*sedentary*	*diligent*	*stoical*	*exasperation*
frugal	*nonchalant*	*pretentious*	*reclusive*	*resilient*

Exercise Two*:* Using Words in Context
- *Fill in the blank with the correct word from the above word bank and underline the context clue.*

1. If you identify yourself with a movie star, you are experiencing _____ pleasure.
2. Since his accident, Jack has been physically inactive, his _____ lifestyle is not healthy.
3. Mary recovered quickly from her illness. Her _____ health was due to the fact that she had always taken care of herself by eating well, getting enough rest, and exercising properly.
4. George always has a calm and casual attitude. His _____ attitude is appreciated by his friends who find him a delight to be around.
5. Terry's combat experiences made him seem more indifferent to emotional pain; however, his _____ attitude was just a cover for the intense emotions he felt since returning from war.
6. The young singer always acted pompous and with much self importance. The audience appreciated his talent but felt that he was _____.
7. It is so irritating and frustrating to continually try to win the race but to persist in coming in second place. It may be my _____ with the race that is preventing me from winning.
8. Ted is very withdrawn, although the other children try to play with him. His teachers are worried that his _____ personality will keep him from forming good social skills.
9. Samuel is such a hardworking young man. His _____ work habits is what earned him his promotion.
10. Wyatt knows how to save money and is always thrifty. Because of his _____ habits, he was able to save almost $4,000 within two months.

Exercise Three: Context clues using Antonyms and Synonyms

Synonyms: Select the word that has the same meaning and write it in the blank.
1. _____   not wasteful, sparing, saving, meticulous
2. _____   anger, annoyance, displeasure, fury, annoyance
3. _____   showing no emotion, indifferent to pain or pleasure

4. _____   pompous, affected, exaggerated, gaudy, showy
5. _____   living one's life through another, serving as a substitute

Antonyms: Select the word with the opposite meaning and write it in the blank

1. _____   active, on the move, migratory
2. _____   not flexible, unbending, not able to rebound
3. _____   friendly, outgoing, participating, sociable, warm
4. _____   worried, concerned, anxious
5. _____   languid, lazy, lethargic, negligent, slack

Exercise Four: Vocabulary - *Circle the correct word*

1. vicarious:
    a) empathic   b) caring   c) tolerant   d) rebellious

2. resilient:
    a) sickly   b) strong   c) inactive   d) outgoing

3. reclusive:
    a) outgoing   b) isolated   c) sociable   d) lethargic

4. stoical:
    a) traditionalist b) displeasure c) pompous d) detached

5. nonchalant:
    a) carefree   b) worried   c) tiresome   d) busy

6. frugal:
    a) saving   b) rebellious   c) gaudy   d) warm

7. sedentary:
    a) defame   b) praise   c) inactive   d) noble

8. diligent:
    a) hardworking   b) lazy   c) boring   d) silly

9. pretentious:
    a) conceited   b) unassuming c) bold   d) brave

10.exasperation:
    a) irritation   b) gentle   c) rage   d) pleasing

Exercise Five: Write the correct form of the word in the blank.

diligent / diligently / diligentness
1. He worked _____ through the night to finish the project.
2. His _____ was appreciated by his boss.
3. He was a _____ person.

vicarious / vicariously / vicariousness
1 .He received _____ pleasure from watching the movie star.
2 .He _____ participated in the world.
3. His _____ was always apparent when he watched movies.

Exercise Six: Word Parts

Refer to your dictionary or thesaurus and write down words that use the following word part on the blank provided

auto	self
brevis	short
eu	well, good
vice	in place of
dis	reversal, apart from,
uni	consisting of one
epi	upon
hypo	under, below
im, in	not
intro	into, within

Literary Terms

1. **Setting:** Surroundings, environment, location, time period in which the action of a novel, play, film, etc., takes place.

2. **Plot:** Storyline, main story of a novel, play, film; the plan, the scheme

3. **Theme:** A unifying dominant idea, motif of a work of art

4. **Protagonist**: Leading character, hero, or heroine, of a drama or other work of art

5. **Antagonist**: A person who is opposed to, struggles against, or competes with another opponent or adversary.

6. **Climax:** The highest or most intense point in the development or resolution of something.

7. **Flashback**: A device of a motion picture, novel, etc., which an event or scene takes place before the present.

8. **Allegory**: Device of using a character and/or story elements symbolically to represent an abstraction in addition to the literal meaning. "The Girl With Large Eyes," is a story about a girl who falls in love with a fish. She and the fish are destroyed because her family does not approve of the marriage. However, it is actually an allegory which has an additional meaning, which shows that prejudice of all kinds is destruction.

9. **Allusion:** A direct or indirect reference to something which is presumably commonly known, such as an event, book, myth, place, or work of art. Example: He is as honest as George Washington.

10. **Analogy**: A similarity or comparison between two different things or the relationship between them. A path or road can sometimes be used as an analogy referencing the different roads or choices we travel through life.

11. **Colloquial**: Everyday speech, the use of slang or informal speech.

12. **Connotation:** The nonliteral associative meaning of a word; the implied, suggested meaning. Example: The word "cool" refers to air temperature being not hot or cold. It also has the connotation of something or one being above average.

13. **Denotation:** Dictionary meaning of a word

14. **Diction:** referring to the style, writer's choice or words, especially with regard to their correctness, clearness, or effectiveness.

15. **Didactic**: From Greek word, literally means "teaching"

16. **Genre:** The major category into which a literary work fits (fiction, drama, non-fiction)

17. **Irony**: The contrast between what is stated explicitly and what is really meant

18. **Metaphor**: A figure of speech using implied comparison of seemingly unlike things or the substitution of one for the other, suggesting some similarity. Example: Love is a rose.

19. **Simile**: A comparison of two things using like or as: Love is like a rose.

20. **Tone**: Similar to mood, describes the author's attitude toward his material, the audience, or both.

21. **Symbol:** Anything that represents or stands for something else: The American flag is a symbol for the U.S.

22. **Imagery:** the sensory details or figurative language used to describe, arouse emotion, or represent abstractions

23. **Apostrophe**: A figure of speech that directly addresses an absent or imaginary person or a person, such as liberty or love. Example: "Oh death where art thou sting."

24. **Personification:** A figure of speech in which the author presents or describes concepts, animals, or inanimate objects by endowing them with human characteristics. Example: The wind spoke with a roaring voice as it uprooted trees and blew down buildings.

25. **Satire:** A work that targets human vices and follies or social institutions and conventions for reform or ridicule. Example: Politicians are often portrayed in cartoons to make a point or to make fun of them.

Literary Terms Worksheet

Setting	Antagonist	Flashback	Allegory	Diction
Climax	Imagery	Symbol	Denotation	Plot
Apostrophe	Irony	Colloquial	Didactic	Protagonist
Genre	Satire	Theme	Analogy	Personification
Simile	Allusion	Metaphor	Tone	Connotation

Write the correct word in the blank:

1. _____ Surroundings, environment, location, time period in which the action of a novel, play, film, etc., takes place.

2. _____ Storyline, main story of a novel, play, film; the plan, the scheme

3. _____ A unifying dominant idea, motif of a work of art

4. _____ Leading character, hero, or heroine, of a drama or other work of art

5. _____ A person who is opposed to, struggles against, or competes with another opponent or adversary.

6. _____ The highest or most intense point in the development or resolution of something.

7. _____ A device of a motion picture, novel, etc., which an event or scene takes place before the present.

8. _____ Device of using a character and/or story elements symbolically to represent an abstraction in addition to the literal meaning. "The Girl With Large Eyes," is a story about a girl who falls in love with a fish. She and the fish are destroyed because her family does not approve of the marriage. However, it is an allegory which actually has an additional meaning which shows that prejudice of all kinds is destruction.

9. _____ A direct or indirect reference to something which is presumably commonly known, such as an event, book, myth, place, or work of art. Example: He is as honest as George Washington.

10. _____ A similarity or comparison between two different things or the relationship between them. A path or road can sometimes be used as an analogy referencing the different roads or choices we travel through life.

11. _____ Everyday speech, the use of slang or informal speech.

12. _____ The nonliteral associative meaning of a word; the implied, suggested meaning. Example: The word "cool" refers to air temperature being not hot or cold. It also has the connotation of something or one being above average.

13. _____ Dictionary meaning of a word

14. _____ Referring to the style, writer's choice or words, especially with regard to their correctness, clearness, or effectiveness.

15. _____ From the Greek word, literally means "teaching"

16. _____ The major category into which a literary work fits (fiction, drama, non-fiction)

17. _____ The contrast between what is stated explicitly and what is really meant

18. _____ A figure of speech using implied comparison of seemingly unlike things or the substitution of one for the other, suggesting some similarity. Example: Love is a rose.

19. _____ A comparison of two things using like or as: Love is like a rose.

20. _____ Similar to mood, describes the author's attitude toward his material, the audience, or both.

21. _____ Anything that represents or stands for something else: The American flag is a symbol for the U.S.

22. _____ The sensory details or figurative language used to describe, arouse emotion, or represent abstractions

23. _____ A figure of speech that directly addresses an absent or imaginary person or a person, such as liberty or love. Example: "Oh death where art thou sting."

24. _____ A figure of speech in which the author presents or describes concepts, animals, or inanimate objects by endowing them with human characteristics. Example: The wind spoke with a roaring voice as it uprooted trees and blew down buildings.

25. _____ A work that targets human vices and follies or social institutions and conventions for reform or ridicule. Example: Politicians are often portrayed in cartoons to make a point or to make fun of them.

Supplement Lists

I have included a section of supplemental information. The vocabulary exercises were designed to help you adapt a formula for learning new vocabulary words. This workbook contains only a fraction of the multitude of words that there for you to use. The supplemental lists give you additional words and information that you should find helpful. I have also included a list of websites that are designed to help with learning grammar.

- *Latin and Greek Derivatives*
- *Confusing Words*
- *Power Verbs*
- *SAT Words*
- *Prepositions*
- *Conjunctions*
- *Websites for Learning Grammar*

Latin-Greek Derivatives

Many of these combining forms may be used as either prefixes or suffixes. Examples are
presented to show current usage.

Prefixes	Derived From:	Meaning	Example
a-, ab-	Latin	off, from, down, away	abduct, avert
a-, an-	Greek	not, without, less	abiotic, anaerobic
actin-	G. aktis	a ray, beam, spoke	actinomycete
ad-	Latin	to, attached to,	adsorption
aer-	Greek	air	aerobic
amphi-	Greek	both, about, around	amphibian
ana-	Latin	away, through, again	analysis
andro-	Greek	man, male	androgens
angio-	Greek	a vessel, closed container	angiospermae
anthropo-	Greek	referring to man	anthropology
ant-, anti-	Greek	against, away, opposite	antibiosis
ante-	Latin	before	anteroom
ap-, aph-, apo-	Latin	from, off, separate	apogee
aqua-	Latin	water	aquatic
arche-, archeo-	Greek	ancient, primitive	archeology
arthri-, arthro-	G. arthron	joint, jointed	arthritis
asco-	G. askos	bag, sack, bladder	ascospore
aureo-	L. aureus	gold colored	aureomycin
auto-	G. autos	self	autoimmune
bi-	Latin	two, twice, double	bipolar, binocular
bio-, bios-	Greek	related to life	biology, biocidal
blasto-	G. blastos	an embryonic layer or cell	blastomere
brachy-	Greek	short	brachycephalic
brad-, brady-	Greek	slow, slowness	bradycardia
bry-, bryo-	G. bryon	moss, mossy	bryophyte
calic-, calix-	Latin	cuplike	calyx
cani-, canis-	Latin	dog	canine
cardia-	G. kardia	heart	cardiac
carn-	L. carnis	flesh	carnivore
carp-	L. carpalis	wrist, bones	carpel
cata-	Greek	decomposition, degradation	catabolism
cell-	L. cella	small room	cellular
cephal-	Latin	head	cephalic
chloro-	G. chloros	green, containing chloride	chlorophyll
chroma-, chromo-	Greek	colored	chromosome

chron-, chrono-	G. chronos	time	chronometer
circum-	Latin	around, near, about	
circumnavigate			
coel-	G. koilos	hollow cavity, belly	coelom
col-, com-, con-	Latin	with, together	combine,
collide			
contra-	Latin	against	contradict
crypto-	G. kryptos	hidden	cryptogamic
cyano-	G. kyanos	dark blue, blue-green	cyanobacteria
cyst-	G. kystis	bladder	cystitis
cyt-,cyte-,cyto-	G. kytos	cell, a hollow vessel	cytology
de-	Latin	undoing, removal of, from	dehydration
den-, dent-	L. dens	tooth	dentition
dendro-	Greek	tree	
dendrochronology			
derm-, derma-	Greek	skin, hide	dermatitis
deut-, deutero-	Greek	second, secondary	deuterium
di-	Greek	double, twice, two	disaccharide
dia-	Greek	through, across	diameter
diplo-	Greek	twofold, double	diploid
dis-	Latin	apart, away	dissolve
dorm-	Latin	to sleep	dormant,
dormitory			
drom-, drome-	Greek	a running, racing	dromendary
e-, ec-	Latin	out, out of	efferent
eco-	G. oikos	house, environment	ecology
ecto-	G. ektos	outside	ectoderm
en-, endo-	G. endon	within, internal	endoskeleton
entero-	G. enteron	intestine	enterocolitis
entomo-	G. entoma	insect	entomology
eo-, eos-	Greek	the dawn	Eocene,
Eohippus			
epi-	Greek	upon, above, top	epidermis
erythro-	Greek	red	erythrocyte
eu-	Greek	proper, true, good	eucaryotic
ex-	Latin	out, from	excise
exo-	Greek	outer, external	
exoskeleton			
extra-	L. exter	outside of, beyond	extracellular
flagell-	L. flagrum	whip, whiplike	flagellum
fuc-, fuco-	G. phyktos	seaweed, algae, lichen	fucoxanthin
gamo-	G. gamos	sexual union	gamogenesis
gastero-,gastro-	G. gaster	stomach, belly	
gastroenteritis			
geno-	L.gene	origin, development	genotype
ge-, geo-	Greek	earth	geology
glu-, glyco-	Greek	sweet, sugar	glucose,
glycogen			
gon-,goni-,gono-	Greek	reproductive, sexual	gonorrhea
gymn-, gymno-	G. gymnos	naked, bare	gymnosperm
gyn-,gyne-,gyno-	Greek	woman, female	gynecology
halo-	G. hals	salt	halophile

haplo-	G. haploos	single	haploid
heme-, hemo-	G. haimo	blood	hemotologist
hemi-	Greek	half	hemisphere
hepta-	Greek	seven	heptane
herb-	L. herba	pertaining to plants	herbicide
hetero-	Greek	different, other, unlike	heterozygous
hex-, hexa-	Greek	six	hexagonal
hipp-, hippo-	G. hippos	horse	hippodrome
histo-	G. histos	tissue	histology
holo-	G. holos	whole, entire	holoblastic
homeo, homo-	Greek	same, similar, like	homogeneous
hyal-, hyalo-	G. hyalos	glassy, transparent	hyaloid
hydr-, hydro-	Greek	pertaining to water	hydrolysis
hyper-	Greek	above, more, over	hyperactive
hypo-	Greek	below, less, under	hypodermic
ichthy-,ichthyo-	Greek	referring to fish	ichthyology
inter-	Latin	between	intercellular
intra-	Latin	within, inside	intracellular
intro-	Latin	inward, within	introvert
iso-	Greek	equal, same	isotonic
kine-	Greek	movement, moving	kinetics
leuc-, leuk-	Greek	white	leucocyte
lycan-	G. lykos	wolf	lycanthropy
macro-	Greek	large, big, long	macromolecule
man-, manu-	Latin	hand	manual
mastig-	G. mastigos	whip	mastigophora
meg-, mega-	Greek	great, large	megabyte
melan-,melano-	Greek	black, dark	melanin
mero-	G. merus	part, piece	meroblast
mes-, meso-	G. mesos	middle, in between	mesoderm
met-, meta-	Greek	later, following, changed	
metamorphosis		in position or form	
micro-	G. mikros	small	microbiology
milli-	Latin	a thousandth part	millimeter
mio-	G. meion	less, smaller	Miocene
mito-	G. mitos	thread	mitosis
mon-, mono-	Greek	one, single	monocular
morph-	Greek	shape, form	morphology
mor-, mort-	Latin	die, death,	mortality
muc-, muco-	Latin	consisting of many units	
multicellular			
mus-	Latin	mouse, as one running	muscle
myco-, mykos-	Greek	fungus, mushroom	mycology
myo-	G. mys	muscle	myoglobin
myxo-	Greek	slime, mucus	myxomycetes
nemato-	Greek	thread, threadlike	nematode
neuro-	Greek	name	nomenclature
ob-	Latin	against	obtuse
octa-	Greek	eight	octopus
olig-, oligo-	Greek	few, small, less	oligarchy
omni-	Latin	all, everywhere	
omnipotent			

oo-	Greek	pertaining to an egg	oocyte
ophthalmo-	Greek	referring to the eye	
ophthalmologist			
opisth-,opistho-	Greek	behind, backwards, back	
Opisthobranchia			
orni-, ornitho-	Greek	bird	ornithology
orth-, ortho-	Greek	straight	orthodontist
osteo-	Greek	bone	osteocyte
oto-	Greek	referring to the ear	otology
ova-,ovi-,ovul-	Latin	egg	ovary,
oviduct			
paleo-	Greek	old, ancient	paleontology
para-	Greek	beside, near, beyond	parasitism
path-, patho-	Greek	disease, suffer	
pathogenic			
ped-, pedi-	Latin	foot	pedicure
penna-, pinna-	Latin	feather, feathery	pinnate
pent-, penta-	Greek	five	pentagon
per-	Latin	through	pervade,
peruse			
peri-	Greek	around, surrounding	perimeter
pher-	Greek	bearing, carrying, support	pheromone
phil- philo-	Greek	loving, attracted to	philanthropy
phob-	Greek	fear, fearing	phobic
photo-	Greek	pertaining to light	
photosynthesis			
phyco-	Greek	seaweed, algae	phycology
phylo-	Greek	tribe, race, related group	phylogeny
phyto-	Greek	pertaining to plants	phytohormone
plasm-, plasma-	Greek	formative substance	plasmablasts
plati-, platy-	Greek	flat	platypus
pleio- pleo-	Greek	more, many	pleiomorphic
pod-,poda-,podi-	Greek	foot	podiatrist
poly-	Greek	many	polyhedron
post-	Latin	after	postnatal
pre-	Latin	before	prenatal
preter-	Latin	beyond	preterhuman
prim-	Latin	first	primary
pro-	Greek	before, on behalf of	proboscis
pro-	Latin	forward	progressive
proto-	Greek	first, primary	protozoa
pseudo-	Greek	false	pseudopod
psilo-	Greek	bare, mere	psilopsida
pteri-, ptero-	Greek	fern, feather	pteridophyte
quadr-, quadri-	Latin	four	quadruped
radi-	Latin	ray, spoke of wheel	radial
re-	Latin	back, again	repeat
retro-	Latin	backward	retroactive
rhiz-, rhizo-	Greek	pertaining to roots	rhizoids
rhod-, rhodo-	Greek	a rose, red	rhodopsin
rota-	Latin	wheel	rotate
sapr-, sapro-	Greek	rotten, putrid, dead	saprobe
sarc-, sarco-	Greek	flesh, fleshy	sarcoma

schiz-, schizo-	Greek	split, splitting	schizocoel
se-	Latin	apart	secede
semi-	Latin	half	semicircle
soma-, somato-	Greek	body	somatic
sperma-,spermato-	Greek	seed	spermatozoa
sporo-	Greek	spore	sporophyte
staphylo-	Greek	bunch of grapes	
staphylococcus			
stoma-	Greek	mouth	stomate
strepto-	Greek	twisted, string of	streptococcus
sub-	Latin	below, under, smaller	subapical
supra-, super-	Latin	above, over	supernova
sym-, syn-	Greek	together, with	synthesis
taxi-, taxo-	Greek	to make order, arrangement	taxonomy
tel-,tele-,telo-	Greek	distant, end	telophase
terra-, terre-	Latin	land, earth	terrestrial
tetra-	Greek	four	tetrapod
therm-, thermo-	Greek	heat	thermometer
thigmo-	Greek	touch	thigmotaxis
trans-	Latin	across, through, over	transfer
tri-	Latin	three	triangle
tricho-	Greek	hair	trichocyst
triplo-	Latin	triple	triploid
troche-, trocho-	Greek	wheel, hoop	trochophore
tropho-	Greek	nourishment	trophoblast
ultra-	Latin	beyond, exceedingly	
ultraconservative			
uni-	Latin	consisting of one	unicellular
vice-	Latin	in place of	vice-
president			
vid-, vis-	Latin	see	vision
xen-, xeno-	Greek	dry, desert	xerophyte
zoo-	Greek	animal, life	zoology
zyg-, zygo-	Greek	to join together	zygote

Suffixes	Derived From:	Meaning	Example
-biosis	Greek	mode of living, way of life	symbiosis
-blast	Greek	formative, embryonic	mesoblast
-chaeta-, -chete	Greek	a bristle	Polychaeta
-chrome	Greek	color	
mercurochrome			
-cidal, -cide	Latin	killer, a killing	insecticide
-cocci, -coccus	Greek	round, seed, kernel	
Streptococcus			
-cyst	Greek	pouch, sac	trichocyst
-dactyl	Greek	finger	pentadactyl
-derm, -dermis	Greek	skin, layer	epidermis
-elle, -ule, -la			

-le, -let, -ole piglet	Latin	small, diminutive endings	globule,
-emia	Greek	blood disease	anemia
-fer conifer, transfer	Latin	bearer, producer, carry	
-gamous, -gamy polygamy	Greek	marriage, sexual fusion	
-gen, -geny hydrogen	Greek	origin, production	progeny,
-genesis embryogenesis	Latin	origin, development of	
-gony	Latin	something produced	cosmogeny
-graph chromatograph	Greek	drawing, writing	
-hedral, -hedron	Greek	side	polyhedral
-hydrate carbohydrate	Greek	compound formed by union of water with other substance	
-ism	Greek	act, practice or result of	terrorism
-ite	Latin	a division or part	somite
-itis appendicitis	Greek	inflammation or infection	
-jugal, -jugate	Latin	to yoke, join together	conjugate
-logy	G. logos	science or study of	biology
-lysis, -lytic	Greek	loosening, separation, splitting into smaller units	photolysis
-mer, -merous	G. meros	a part, piece	polymer
-meter	G. metron	a measurement	diameter
-morph	Greek	form	endomorph
-mycin	Greek	derived from a fungus	aureomycin
-nomy	Greek	systematized knowledge of	astronomy
-oma	Greek	tumorous	carcinoma
-osis, -otic	Greek	abnormal condition, disease	neurosis
-phage bacteriophage	Greek	eater	
-phase	Greek	a stage or condition	metaphase
-phil, -phile	Greek	fear, fearing	hydrophobia
-phor, -phore sporangiophore	Greek	bearing, carrying, supporting	
-phyll	Greek	leaf	chorophyll
-phyta, -phyte	Greek	plant	epiphyte
-plasm	Greek	formative substance	cytoplasm
-plast	Greek	organized particle, granule	choroplast
-pod, -poda	Greek	foot	arthropod
-some	Greek	body	chromosome
-stasis	Greek	a stationary position	homeostasis

-stat, -static	Greek	stationary, still	hemostat
-stomy	Greek	opening into	colostomy
-therm	Greek	heat	homeotherm
-thes, -thesis	Greek	arrangement, in order	hypothesis
-tom, -tomy	Greek	dividing, surgery	lobotomy
-trope, -tropic	Greek	turning	phototropic
-vor, -vore	L. vorare	feeding	carnivore
-zoa,-zoan,-zoic	Greek	animal, life	protozoa

Confusing Words

- ALL READY-prepared
  Dinner was all ready when the guests arrived.

  ALREADY-by this time
  The turkey was already burned when the guests arrived.

- ALTOGETHER-entirely
  Altogether, I thought that the student's presentation was well planned.

  ALL TOGETHER-gathered, with everything in one place
  We were all together at the family reunion last spring.

- APART-to be separated
  The chain-link fence kept the angry dogs apart. OR My old car fell apart before we reached California.

  A PART-to be joined with
  The new course was a part of the new field of study at the university. OR A part of this plan involves getting started at dawn.

- ASCENT- climb
  The plane's ascent made my ears pop.

  ASSENT-agreement
  The martian assented to undergo experiments.

- BREATH-noun, air inhaled or exhaled
  You could see his breath in the cold air.

  BREATHE-verb, to inhale or exhale
  If you don't breathe, then you are dead.

- CAPITAL-seat of government. Also financial resources.
  The capital of Virginia is Richmond.

  The firm had enough capital to build the new plant.

  CAPITOL-the actual building in which the legislative body meets
  The governor announced his resignation in a speech given at the capitol today.

- CITE-to quote or document
  I cited ten quotes from the same author in my paper.

  SIGHT-vision
  The sight of the American flag arouses different emotions in different parts of the world.

  SITE-position or place
  The new office building was built on the site of a cemetary.

- COMPLEMENT-noun, something that completes; verb, to complete
A nice dry white wine complements a seafood entree.

  COMPLIMENT-noun, praise; verb, to praise
The professor complimented Betty on her proper use of a comma.

- CONSCIENCE-sense of right and wrong
The student's conscience kept him from cheating on the exam.

  CONSCIOUS-awake
I was conscious when the burglar entered the house.

- COUNCIL-a group that consults or advises
The men and women on the council voted in favor of an outdoor concert in their town.

  COUNSEL-to advise
The parole officer counseled the convict before he was released.

- ELICIT-to draw or bring out
The teacher elicited the correct response from the student.

  ILLICIT-illegal
The Columbian drug lord was arrested for his illicit activities.

- EMINENT-famous, respected
The eminent podiatrist won the Physician of the Year award.

  IMMANENT-inherent or intrinsic
The meaning of the poem was immanent, and not easily recognized.

  IMMINENT-ready to take place
A fight between my sister and me is imminent from the moment I enter my house.

- ITS-of or belonging to it
The baby will scream as soon as its mother walks out of the room.

  IT'S-contraction for it is
It's a beautiful day in the neighborhood.

- LEAD-noun, a type of metal
Is that pipe made of lead?

  LED-verb, past tense of the verb "to lead"
She led the campers on an over-night hike.

- LIE-to lie down (a person or animal. *hint: people can tell lies*)
I have a headache, so I'm going to lie down for a while.

  (also lying, lay, has/have lain—The dog has lain in the shade all day; yesterday, the dog lay there for twelve hours).
- LAY-to lay an object down.
"Lay down that gun, Bubba!" The sheriff demanded.
The town lay at the foot of the mountain.

  (also laying, laid, has/have laid—At that point, Bubba laid the gun on the ground).

- LOSE—verb, to misplace or not win
  Mom glared at Mikey. "If you lose that new lunchbox, don't even think of coming home!"

  LOOSE—noun, to not be tight; verb (rarely used)—to release
  The burglar's pants were so loose that he was sure to lose the race with the cop chasing him.
  While awaiting trial, he was never set loose from jail because no one would post his bail.

- NOVEL-noun, a book that is a work of fiction. Do not use "novel" for nonfiction; use "book" or "work."
  Mark Twain wrote his novel *Adventures of Huckleberry Finn* when he was already well known, but before he published many other works of fiction and nonfiction.

- PASSED-verb, past tense of "to pass," to have moved
  The tornado passed through the city quickly, but it caused great damage.

  PAST-belonging to a former time or place
  Who was the past president of Microsquish Computers?

- Go past the fire station and turn right.

- PRECEDE-to come before
  Pre-writing precedes the rough draft of good papers.

  PROCEED-to go forward
  He proceeded to pass back the failing grades on the exam.

- PRINCIPAL-adjective, most important; noun, a person who has authority
  The principal ingredient in chocolate chip cookies is chocolate chips.

  The principal of the school does the announcements each morning.

  PRINCIPLE-a general or fundamental truth
  The study was based on the principle of gravity.

- QUOTE-verb, to cite
  I would like to quote Dickens in my next paper.

  QUOTATION-noun, the act of citing
  The book of famous quotations inspired us all.

- STATIONARY-standing still
  The accident was my fault because I ran into a stationary object.

  STATIONERY-writing paper
  My mother bought me stationery that was on recycled paper.

- SUPPOSED TO-correct form for "to be obligated to" or "presumed to" NOT "suppose to"

  SUPPOSE-to guess or make a conjecture
  Do you <u>suppose</u> we will get to the airport on time? When is our plane <u>supposed to</u> arrive? We are <u>supposed to</u> check our bags before we board, but I <u>suppose</u> we could do that at the curb and save time.

- THAN-use with comparisons
  I would rather go out to eat than eat at the dining hall.

THEN-at that time, or next
I studied for my exam for seven hours, and then I went to bed.

- THEIR-possessive form of they
Their house is at the end of the block.

THERE-indicates location (hint: think of "here and there")
There goes my chance of winning the lottery!

THEY'RE-contraction for "they are"
They're in Europe for the summer—again!

- THROUGH-by means of; finished; into or out of
He plowed right through the other team's defensive line.

THREW-past tense of throw
She threw away his love love letters.

THOROUGH-careful or complete
John thoroughly cleaned his room; there was not even a speck of dust when he finished.

THOUGH-however; nevertheless
He's really a sweetheart though he looks tough on the outside.

THRU-abbreviated slang for through; not appropriate in standard writing
We're thru for the day!

- TO-toward
I went to the University of Richmond.

TOO-also, or excessively
He drank too many screwdrivers and was unable to drive home.

TWO-a number
Only two students did not turn in the assignment.

- WHO-pronoun, referring to a person or persons
Jane wondered how Jack, who is so smart, could be having difficulties in Calculus.

WHICH-pronoun, replacing a singular or plural thing(s);not used to refer to persons
Which section of history did you get into?

THAT-used to refer to things or a group or class of people
I lost the book that I bought last week.

- WHO-used as a subject or as a subject complement (see above)
John is the man who can get the job done.

WHOM-used as an object
Whom did Sarah choose as her replacement

Power Verbs

A
abated
abbreviated
abolished
abridged
absolved
absorbed
accelerated
accentuated
accommodated
accomplished
accounted for
accrued
accumulated
achieved
acquired
acted
adapted
adopted
added
addressed
adjusted
administered
advanced
advertised
advised
advocated
affirmed
aided
alerted
aligned
allayed
alleviated
allocated
allotted
altered
amassed
amended
analyzed
answered
anticipated
appeased
applied
appointed
appraised
approached
appropriated
approved
arbitrated
aroused
arranged
articulated

delivered
demonstrated
deployed
derived
described
designated
designed
detailed
detected
determined
developed
devised
diagnosed
differentiated
diffused
directed
disbursed
discovered
discussed
dispatched
dispensed
displayed
disposed
disproved
dissected
disseminated
dissolved
distinguished
distributed
diversified
diverted
divested
divided
documented
doubled
drafted
dramatized
drew up
drove

E
earned
eased
economized
edited
educated
effected
elaborated
elected
elevated
elicited
eliminated

invented
inventoried
invested
investigated
invigorated
invited
involved
isolated
issued
itemized

J
joined
judged
justified

L
launched
learned
lectured
led
lessened
leveraged
licensed
lifted
limited
linked
liquidated
listened
litigated
loaded
located
logged

M
made
maintained
managed
mandated
maneuvered
manipulated
manufactured
mapped
marked
marketed
mastered
maximized
measured
mediated
memorized
mentored
merged

rehabilitated
reinforced
reiterated
related
released
relied
relieved
remained
remodeled
rendered
renegotiated
renewed
reorganized
repaired
replaced
replied
replicated
reported
represented
reproduced
requested
researched
reserved
resolved
responded
restored
restructured
retained
retooled
retrieved
returned
revamped
reversed
reviewed
revised
revitalized
revolutionized
rewarded
risked
rotated
routed

S
safeguarded
salvaged
saved
scanned
scheduled
screened
sculptured
searched
secured

ascertained
aspired
assembled
assessed
assigned
assimilated
assisted
assured
attained
attended
audited
augmented
authored
authorized
automated
averted
avoided
awarded

B
balanced
began
benchmarked
benefited
bid
billed
blended
blocked
bolstered
boosted
bought
branded
bridged
broadened
brought
budgeted
built

C
calculated
calibrated
capitalized
captured
cared for
carried
carved
categorized
catalogued
caught
cautioned
cemented
certified
chaired
challenged
championed

embraced
emphasized
empowered
enabled
encouraged
ended
enforced
engaged
engineered
enhanced
enlisted
enriched
enrolled
ensured
entered
entertained
enticed
equipped
established
estimated
evaluated
examined
exceeded
executed
exercised
exhibited
expanded
expedited
experienced
experimented
explained
explored
expressed
extended
extracted

F
fabricated
facilitated
factored
familiarized
fashioned
fielded
filed
filled
finalized
financed
fine tuned
finished
fixed
focused
followed
forecasted
forged
formalized

merited
met
minimized
mobilized
modeled
moderated
modified
molded
monitored
monopolized
motivated
mounted
moved
multiplied

N
named
narrated
navigated
negotiated
netted
neutralized
nominated
normalized
notified
nurtured

O
observed
obtained
offered
officiated
offset
opened
operated
optimized
orchestrated
ordered
organized
oriented
originated
outdistanced
outlined
outperformed
overcame
overhauled
oversaw
owned

P
paced
packaged
packed
pared
participated

seized
selected
sent
separated
sequenced
served
serviced
set up
settled
shaped
shared
sharpened
shipped
shortened
showed
signed
simplified
simulated
sketched
slashed
smoothed
solicited
sold
solidified
solved
sorted
sourced
sparked
spearheaded
specialized
specified
speculated
spent
spoke
sponsored
spurred
staffed
standardized
started
steered
stimulated
streamlined
strengthened
stretched
structured
studied
submitted
succeeded
suggested
summarized
supervised
supplied
supported
surpassed
surveyed

changed
charged
charted
checked
chose
chronicled
circulated
circumvented
cited
clarified
classified
cleaned
cleared
closed
coached
coded
collaborated
collated
collected
combined
commanded
commended
commenced
commissioned
communicated
compared
compiled
complemented
completed
complied
composed
compounded
computed
conceived
concentrated
conceptualized
condensed
conducted
conferred
configured
confirmed
confronted
connected
conserved
considered
consolidated
constructed
consulted
consummated
contacted
continued
contracted
contributed
controlled
converted

formed
formulated
fortified
forwarded
fostered
fought
found
founded
framed
fulfilled
functioned as
funded
furnished
furthered

G
gained
garnered
gathered
gauged
gave
generated
governed
graduated
grasped
greeted
grew
grouped
guaranteed
guided

H
halted
halved
handled
headed
heightened
held
helped
hired
honed
hosted
hypnotized
hypothesized

I
identified
ignited
illustrated
implemented
imported
improved
improvised
incited
included

partnered
passed
penetrated
perceived
perfected
performed
persuaded
photographed
piloted
pinpointed
pioneered
placed
planned
played
praised
predicted
prepared
prescribed
presented
preserved
presided
prevailed
prevented
printed
prioritized
processed
procured
produced
profiled
programmed
progressed
projected
promoted
proofread
proposed
protected
proved
provided
pruned
publicized
purchased
pursued

Q
quadrupled
qualified
quantified
queried
questioned
quoted

R
raised
rallied
ranked

swayed
swept
symbolized
synthesized
systemized

T
tabulated
tackled
talked
tallied
targeted
tasted
taught
teamed
tempered
tended
terminated
tested
testified
tied
took
topped
totaled
traced
tracked
trained
transcribed
transformed
transitioned
translated
transmitted
traveled
treated
trimmed
tripled
troubleshot
turned
tutored
typed

U
uncovered
underlined
underscored
undertook
underwrote
unearthed
unified
united
updated
upgraded
upheld
urged
used

conveyed
convinced
cooperated
coordinated
copied
corrected
corresponded
counseled
created
critiqued
cultivated
customized
cut

D
dealt
debated
debugged
decided
decoded
decreased
dedicated
defined
delegated
delineated

incorporated
increased
indicated
individualized
indoctrinated
induced
influenced
informed
infused
initiated
innovated
inspected
inspired
installed
instilled
instituted
instructed
insured
integrated
intensified
interacted
interceded
interpreted
intervened
interviewed

rated
reached
read
realigned
realized
rearranged
reasoned
rebuilt
received
recognized
recommended
reconciled
reconstructed
recorded
recovered
recruited
rectified
redesigned
redirected
reduced
re-engineered
referred
refocused
registered
regulated

utilized

V
validated
valued
vaulted
verbalized
verified
viewed
visualized
voiced
volunteered

W
weathered
weighed
widened
withstood
won
worked
wove
wrote

Y
yielded

Group 1

Abhor	hate
Bigot	narrow-minded, prejudiced person
Counterfeit	fake; false
Enfranchise	give voting rights
Hamper	hinder; obstruct
Kindle	to start a fire
Noxious	harmful; poisonous; lethal
Placid	calm; peaceful
Remuneration	payment for work done
Talisman	lucky charm

Group 2

Abrasive	rough; coarse; harsh
Bilk	cheat; defraud
Covert	hidden; undercover
Engender	cause
Hangar	storage area (like garage) for a plane

Knotty	complex; difficult to solve
Nuance	something subtle; a fine shade of meaning
Plagiarism	taking credit for someone else's writing or ideas
Renown	Fame
Tangent	going off the main subject

Group 3

Abasement	humiliation; degradation
Billowing	swelling; fluttering; waving
Cower	recoil in fear or servility; shrink away from
Enhance	improve; make better or clearer
Harangue	noisy, attacking speech
Labyrinth	a maze
Nullify	to counter; make unimportant
Plaintiff	petitioner (in court of law)
Replete	Full
Tangible	can be touched

Group 4

Abrogate	cancel; deny; repeal

Blasphemy	speech which offends religious sentiments
Credible	Believable
Enigma	puzzle; mystery
Harbingers	indicators; bringers of warnings
Labyrinthine	complicated; highly convoluted
Nuzzle	cuddle; snuggle
Plaudit	statement giving strong praise
Reprehensible	shameful; very bad
Tardy	slow; late; overdue; delayed

Group 5

Absolution	forgiveness; pardon; release
Blatant	Obvious
Creditable	Praiseworthy
Ensconce	establish firmly in a position
Hasten	hurry; accelerate; rush
Laceration	a cut
Obdurate	Stubborn
Plausible	can be believed; reasonable
Reprieve	a respite; postponement of a sentence

Tawdry	of little value; gaudy

Group 6

Abstain	desist; go without; withdraw
Blighted	damaged; destroyed; ruined
Credulous	gullible; ready to believe anything
Enshroud	Cover
Haughtiness	arrogance; pride
Lachrymose	tearful; sad
Obfuscate	deliberately make something difficult to understand
Plethora	an excess
Repudiate	shun; eschew
Tedium	Boredom

Group 7

Abstemious	self denying; refraining from indulging
Blithe	free-spirited; carefree
Crepuscular	active at dawn and dusk
Enunciation	clear pronunciation; accent; articulation
Headstrong	stubborn; willful

Lackluster	dull; monotonous; bland
Objective	unbiased; not subjective
Pliable	flexible; not stubborn
Rescind	retract; repeal
Temper	to moderate; soften

Group 8

Abstruse	difficult to understand; obscure
Blunderbuss	1. ancient weapon (type of gun); 2. a clumsy person
Cringe	recoil; flinch; shy away
Envenom	to cause bitterness and bad feeling
Hedonism	self indulgence; pleasure-seeking
Laconic	using few words; brief; to the point
Oblique	indirect; slanting
Plumage	feathers of a bird
Resignation	acceptance of fate
Tenacious	stubborn; resolute; holding firm to a purpose

Group 9

Accolade	tribute; honor; praise

Bolster	support; prop up
Cryptic	puzzling; enigmatic
Ephemeral	short-lived
Hedonist	a pleasure seeker
Lamentation	expression of regret or sorrow
Obliterate	destroy; demolish; eradicate
Plummet	fall suddenly and steeply
Resolution	Determination
Tentative	not certain

Group 10

Acquiesce	to agree to; give in to
Bombast	arrogant, pompous language
Curtail	cut short
Epicure	someone who appreciates good food and drink
Heed	listen to
Lampoon	ridicule; spoof
Oblivious	totally unaware
Podium	raised platform
Resonant	Echoing

| Tenuous | flimsy; not solid |

Word List Two

Group 1

Acrid	sharp; pungent (used of smells and tastes)
Boorish	ill-mannered
Cynical	believing that people act only out of selfish motives
Epistle	a letter (form of communication)
Heresy	against orthodox opinion
Lance	spear; spike; javelin
Obscure	difficult to understand; partially hidden
Poignant	deeply moving; strongly affecting the emotions
Respite	a break; intermission
Terse	concise; to the point

Group 2

Acrophobia	fear of heights
Bourgeois	middle class
Debility	weakness; incapacity
Epistolary	concerned with letters; through correspondence

Hiatus	interruption; pause
Languid	tired; slow
Obscured	hidden; covered; buried
Poised	calm; collected; self-possessed
Resplendent	shining; glowing
Therapeutic	medicinal; curative

Group 3

Acuity	sharpness (mental or visual)
Braggart	someone who boasts
Debunking	exposing false claims or myths
Epitomized	typified; characterized; personified
Hidebound	rigid in opinions
Languish	decay; fade away; get weaker
Obsequious	servile; submissive
Polemical	causing debate or argument
Restorative	a tonic
Thwart	prevent; frustrate

Group 4

Adamant	forceful; inflexible
Brawny	Muscular
Decathlon	an athletic competition with ten events
Equivocate	speak ambiguously; avoid telling the truth
Hieroglyphics	1. picture writing; 2. writing which is difficult to read or enigmatic
Larceny	theft; robbery; stealing
Obsession	a dominating concern
Ponderous	weighty; slow and heavy
Retention	preservation; withholding
Timorous	cowardly; fearful

Group 5

Adroit	Skilful
Brevity	being brief
Decorum	dignified, correct behavior [decorous (a)]
Err	make a mistake
Hinder	Obstruct
Largess	Generosity

Obsolete	no longer valid
Pontificate	speak pompously or dogmatically
Reticent	restrained; holding something back; uncommunicative
Tirade	stream of verbal abuse

Group 6

Adulation	strong admiration; worship
Bristle	to show irritation
Decoy	lure; trap; trick
Erratic	wandering; irregular
Histrionic	theatrical; exaggerated
Laud	Praise
Obstreperous	noisy and boisterous
Portend	Foretell
Retraction	withdrawal; cancellation of a statement
Titter	giggle quietly

Group 7

Adversity	Hardship

Broach	start to discuss; approach
Deference	Respect
Esoteric	obscure and difficult to understand
Hoary	Old
Lavish	on a grand scale; wasteful
Obtuse	mentally dull
Portent	a warning sign; omen
Revere	Worship
Tome	large book

Group 8

Advocate	Support
Brusque	blunt; abrupt
Defoliate	cause leaves to fall off
Espouse	promote; take up; support
Hone	sharpen; increase; whet
Lax	careless; not strict
Obviate	avoid; make unnecessary
Poseur	someone who puts on an act
Riddled	full of (usually full of holes)

Torpid	inactive; lazy; stagnant

Group 9

Aesthetic	concerning art or beauty
Bulwark	fortification; barricade; wall
Defunct	no longer in existence
Etymology	the study of word origins
Hyperbole	grossly exaggerated speech
Legend	1. key to map; 2. myth or story
Odious	Hateful
Posterity	future generations
Rife	Common
Torpor	dormancy; sluggishness; inactivity

Group 10

Affable	friendly; social; easygoing
Bureaucracy	Officialdom
Degradation	deprivation; poverty; debasement
Eulogy	Praise
Hypochondriac	a person obsessed with health; having imaginary

	illnesses
Legion	in large numbers
Officious	domineering; intrusive; meddlesome
Posthumous	after death
Rigor	Thoroughness
Totter	walk unsteadily

Word List Three

Group 1

Ambivalence	lack of clarity; wavering; being undecided
Cantankerous	bad-tempered; quarrelsome
Derogatory	Uncomplimentary
Exemplify	to serve as a good example
Impecunious	having no money
Lucid	Clear
Ornate	highly decorated
Precipice	steep slope
Salubrious	health-giving
Truant	shirker; someone absent without permission

Group 2

Ambulatory	able to walk around (used of hospital patients)
Capacious	Spacious
Desecrate	to damage or pollute a holy place
Exhaustive	complete and thorough
Impious	wicked; profane
Ludicrous	ridiculous; silly
Orthodox	Conventional
Precipitous	done in a hurry
Salutary	something which teaches you a lesson; beneficial
Truncate	cut short

Group 3

Ameliorate	make better
Capitulate	surrender; give in to
Desecration	spoiling something holy
Exonerates	acquits; absolves; removes blame
Impoverished	destitute; poor
Lukewarm	1. unenthusiastic; 2. neither hot nor cold
Ossify	1. turn to bone; 2. become fixed and rigid

Preclude	prevent or make impossible
Sanctimonious	hypocritically holy
Tumult	uproar; noise

Group 4

Amelioration	Improvement
Carping	constant criticism
Desist	stop; discontinue; cease
Exorcism	getting free/rid of; eliminating (especially demons)
Impromptu	unrehearsed; spontaneous
Lummox	clumsy person
Ostentatious	Showy
Precocious	developing early
Sanction	give approval to
Turpitude	Depravity

Group 5

Amiable	Friendly
Cartographer	person who makes maps
Despondent	having no hope; miserable

Expatriate	refugee; emigrant; someone living away from his own country
Inadvertent	not intentional
Luscious	juicy; moist; succulent
Oust	push out of a position
Predecessor	one who came before
Sanguinary	bloodthirsty; bloody
Tyro	novice; beginner

Group 6

Amity	Friendship
Castigate	scold strongly
Destitution	hardship; poverty; misery
Expedient	convenient; practical
Incantation	chant; invocation; prayer
Lynch	assassinate; kill; illegal hanging
Overt	obvious; not hidden
Predicament	dilemma; difficult situation
Sanguine	optimistic; cheerful
Ubiquitous	found everywhere; omnipresent

Group 7

Amorphous	lacking in shape
Catharsis	purging of pent-up emotions
Deter	put off; prevent
Expedite	make faster
Incarceration	putting in prison
Machinations	plots and plans
Overwrought	worked up; in an emotional state
Preeminent	famous; outstanding
Sardonic	Mocking
Unalloyed	undiluted; total

Group 8

Analgesic	medicine to combat pain
Caucus	type of private political meeting
Deteriorate	worsen; decline
Exposition	clear explanation
Incessant	without stopping
Maelstrom	whirlpool; storm in the ocean

Palatable	good to eat; agreeable
Prerogative	right or privilege
Savant	person with knowledge
Unctuous	oily; using excessive flattery

Group 9

Analogous	Comparable
Caustic	Burning
Detrimental	Harmful
Extol	Praise
Incipient	just beginning
Magnanimous	generous; big-hearted
Palisade	fence made of posts
Prescient	having fore-knowledge
Scale	to climb
Undermined	damaged; attacked

Group 10

Anarchy	chaos; lack of government
Cavalcade	procession of vehicles
Devoured	greedily eaten/consumed

Extradite	deport from one country back to the home country
Inclination	tendency; a leaning toward
Magnate	powerful businessman
Palliative	a remedy that improves but doesn't cure
Presentiment	a feeling that something might happen
Scapegoat	person on whom blame is placed for faults of others
Underscore	Emphasize

Prepositions

A Preposition is a word that relates a noun or pronoun to another word in a sentence.
"The dog sat <u>under</u> the tree"

about	behind	From	on	toward
above	below	In	on top of	under
across	beneath	in front of	onto	underneath
after	beside	Inside	out of	until
against	between	instead of	outside	up
along	by	into	over	upon
among	down	like	past	with
around	during	near	since	within
at	except	of	through	without
before	for	off	to	

COORDINATING CONJUNCTIONS

F	A	N	B	O	Y	S
for	and	nor	but	or	yet	so

An easy way to remember these six conjunctions is to think of the word FANBOYS. Each of the letters in this somewhat unlikely word is the first letter of one of the coordinating conjunctions. Remember, when using a conjunction to join two sentences, use a comma before the conjunction.

EXAMPLES AND SENTENCES
COORDINATING CONJUNCTIONS

CONJUNCTION	WHAT IS LINKED	SAMPLE SENTENCES
and	noun phrase+noun phrase	We have tickets for the symphony **and** the opera.
but	sentence+sentence	The orchestra rehearses on Tuesday, **but** the chorus rehearses on Wednesday.
or	verb+verb	Have you seen **or** heard the opera by Scott Joplin?
so	sentence+sentence	I wanted to sit in the front of the balcony, **so** I ordered my tickets early.

CORRELATIVE CONJUNCTIONS

both...and	not only...but also	either...or	neither...nor	whether...or

Remember, correlative conjunctions are always used in pairs. They join similar elements. When joining singular and plural subjects, the subject closest to the verb determines whether the verb is singular or plural.

EXAMPLES AND SENTENCES
CORRELATIVE CONJUNCTIONS

CONJUNCTIONS	WHAT IS LINKED	SAMPLE SENTENCE
both...and	subject+subject	**Both** my sister **and** my brother play the piano.
either...or	noun+noun	Tonight's program is **either** Mozart **or** Beethoven.
neither...nor	subject+subject	**Neither** the orchestra **nor** the chorus was able to

		overcome the terrible acoustics in the church
not only...but also	sentence+sentence	**Not only** does Sue raise money for the symphony, **but she also** ushers at all of their concerts.

SUBORDINATING CONJUNCTIONS

TIME	CAUSE + EFFECT	OPPOSITION	CONDITION
after	because	although	if
before	since	though	unless
when	now that	even though	only if
while	as	whereas	whether or not
since	in order that	while	even if
until	so		in case (that)

Subordinating conjunctions, (subordinators) are most important in creating subordinating clauses. These adverbs that act like conjunctions are placed at the front of the clause. The adverbial clause can come either before or after the main clause. Subordinators are usually a single word, but there are also a number of multi-word subordinators that function like a single subordinating conjunction. They can be classified according to their use in regard to time, cause and effect, opposition, or condition. Remember, put a comma at the end of the adverbial phrase when it precedes the main clause.

EXAMPLES AND SENTENCES
SUBORDINATING CONJUNCTIONS

CONJUNCTION	SAMPLE SENTENCE
after	We are going out to eat **after** we finish taking the test.
since	**Since** we have lived in Atlanta, we have gone to every exhibit at the High Musuem.
while	**While** I was waiting in line for the Matisse Exhibit, I ate my lunch.
although	**Although** the line was long and the wait over two hours, the exhibit was well worth it
even if	**Even if** you have already bought your ticket, you will still need to wait in line.
because	I love Matisse's works **because** he uses color so brilliantly.

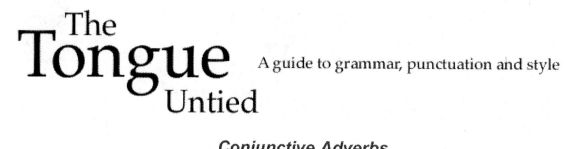

Conjunctive Adverbs

Conjunctive adverbs are not true conjunctions, but these adverbs often function as conjunctions in joining two <u>independent</u> clauses.

They serve as transitional devices between one main thought and another.

Common Conjunctive Adverbs:	
Accordingly	Afterwards
Also	Consequently
However	Indeed
Likewise	Moreover
Nevertheless	Nonetheless
Otherwise	Similarly
So*	Still
Therefore	
(*may also be subordinating)	

NOTE: Because conjunctive adverbs are not true conjunctions, a semicolon is required when connecting two independent clauses.

Conjunctive adverbs other than SO or OTHERWISE require a semicolon preceding them and a comma following them.

- The president will be attending the lecture; **accordingly**, the vice president will be available for the luncheon.
  - The two clauses are independent. The semicolon replaces a coordinating conjunction and indicates that the two clauses are independent.

- Jaime wanted to see "Mission Impossible"; **however**, Nick wanted to see "28 Days."
    - The two clauses are independent. The semicolon replaces a coordinating conjunction and indicates that the two clauses are independent.

SO and OTHERWISE do not require a comma following them when they are Conjunctive adverbs.

- The best candidate for the job missed her flight; **so** we will postpone the interviews until tomorrow.
    - Remember, for SO to be a subordinating conjunction the meaning must be IN ORDER THAT or WITH THE PURPOSE THAT. To be a coordinating conjunction SO must mean DURING THE TIME THAT. When the meaning of SO is THEREFORE, it is a conjunctive adverb.

- You will need to focus on the goal; **otherwise** it is easy to get distracted.
    - The two clauses are independent. The semicolon replaces a coordinating conjunction and indicates that the two clauses are independent, but no comma is required after OTHERWISE.

A conjunctive adverb connects two ideas (independent clauses). If the above words interrupt a thought, they are not conjunctive adverbs and are not punctuated as such (Weinhold).

RESOURCES:

- Azar, B. S.(1993). *Understanding and Using English Grammar*. Englewood Hills, NJ: Prentice Hall Regents.
- Byrd, P. and Benson, B. (1992). *Applied English Grammar*. Boston: Heinle & Heinle.
- Greenbaum, S. and Quirk, R. (1990). *A Student's Grammar of the English Language*. Essex, England: Longman.
- Hodges, J. and Whitten, M. (1984). *Harbrace College Handbook*. Atlanta: Harcourt Brace

Website for Help with Grammar and Vocabulary:

1. *Owl at Purdue*: http://owl.english.purdue.edu/ - This website has information on the following: (Excellent Site)

- Writing
- Research
- Grammar and Mechanics
- Style Guides
- ESL (English as a Second Language)
- Job Search and Professional Writing

2. The Tongue United, "A Guide to Grammar, Punctuation, and Style," Kellie Weinhold, was developed by Kellie Weinhold as support for a course offered to all pre-majors in the School of Journalism and Communication at the University of Oregon. *Excellent site -* has quizzes, tests, etc. and is extremely organized.

3. *Guide to Grammar and Writing*: http://grammar.ccc.commnet.edu/grammar/

4. *English Grammar Help*: http://esl.about.com/od/englishgrammar/English Grammar Help Rules Worksheets Games Quizzes Exercises.htm

5. *Grammar Help*: http://www.cfcc.edu/rmorris/grammar.html

6. *English Grammar Help (SAT/ACT)*: http://grammarmechanics.org/

Works Cited

American Heritage Dictionary. 2nd College ed. Boston: Houghton Miffin Co, 1982.

"Commonly Confused Words." Writer's Web, 04 June 08

 < http://writing2.richmond.edu/WRITING/wweb/conford.html>.

Bryson, Linda. "English Conjunction." 08 June 08

 <http://www2.gsu.edu/~wwwesl/egw/bryson.htm#COORDINATING>.

Harper, Douglas. "Online Etymology." 03 June 08 <http://www.etymonline.com/index.php?l=b>.

"Latin and Greek Derivative." 04 June 08

 <http://www.angelfire.com/de/nestsite/modbiogreek.html>.

Power Verb. 08 June 2008 <http://www.webresume.com/resumes/verbs.html>.

Rickerson, E.M. "Are Dialects Dying in the US?" "Talkin' About Talk."

 College of Charleston, Charleston, SC. 2004. 08 June 08

 <http://www.cofc.edu/linguist/archives/2005/04/are_dialects_dy_1.html>.

SAT Prep. 04 June 08 <http://www.majortests.com/sat/wordlist.php>.

Schrock Earl F. Jr. *The Patterns of English Grammar, Discovering the Patterns in English*

 Grammar through Analysis of One's Own Speech and Writing. Russellville: ATU.

Weinhold, Kellie. "Tongue United." "A Guide to Grammar Punctuation and Style." 08 June 2008

 <http://grammar.uoregon.edu/intro.html>.

Young Frankenstein. Mel Brooks. Perf. Gene Wilder, Peter Boyle, Marty Feldman, Teri Garr,
Madeline

 Kahn, Cloris Lechman. DVD. 20th Century Fox Home Entertainment, 1998.